Jossey-Bass Teacher

Jossey-Bass Teacher provides K–12 teachers with essential knowledge and tools to create a positive and lifelong impact on student learning. Trusted and experienced educational mentors offer practical classroom-tested and theory-based teaching resources for improving teaching practice in a broad range of grade levels and subject areas. From one educator to another, we want to be your first source to make every day your best day in teaching. *Jossey-Bass Teacher* resources serve two types of informational needs—essential knowledge and essential tools.

Essential knowledge resources provide the foundation, strategies, and methods from which teachers may design curriculum and instruction to challenge and excite their students. Connecting theory to practice, essential knowledge books rely on a solid research base and time-tested methods, offering the best ideas and guidance from many of the most experienced and well-respected experts in the field.

Essential tools save teachers time and effort by offering proven, ready-to-use materials for in-class use. Our publications include activities, assessments, exercises, instruments, games, ready reference, and more. They enhance an entire course of study, a weekly lesson, or a daily plan. These essential tools provide insightful, practical, and comprehensive materials on topics that matter most to K–12 teachers.

The Substitute Teaching
SURVIVAL GUIDE

Emergency Lesson Plans and Essential Advice

GRADES K–5

JOHN DELLINGER

 JOSSEY-BASS
A Wiley Imprint
www.josseybass.com

Published by Jossey-Bass
A Wiley Imprint
989 Market Street, San Francisco, CA 94103-1741   www.josseybass.com

ISBN-10 0-7879-7410-2
ISBN-13 978-0-7879-7410-7

Jossey-Bass books and products are available through most bookstores. To contact Jossey-Bass directly, call our Customer Care Department within the U.S. at 800-956-7739, outside the U.S. at 317-572-3986, or fax 317-572-4002.

Jossey-Bass also publishes its books in a variety of electronic formats. Some content that appears in print may not be available in electronic books.

Printed in the United States of America
FIRST EDITION
PB Printing   10 9 8 7 6 5 4 3 2 1

About the Book

When teachers are absent from their classrooms, substitute teachers are sometimes left with no directions, no lesson plans, and no way to control the kids. How can a substitute teacher maintain order in the classroom, much less engage the students in a meaningful learning experience?

While most books for substitute teachers offer tips and suggestions for classroom management, this unique volume also provides an even more important resource: 144 emergency lesson plans for grades K through 5. With a multitude of useful suggestions and 24 learning exercises for each grade level, this book is an essential tool for both the novice and the experienced substitute teacher and a perfect resource as well for regular teachers who wish to plan ahead for their absence.

This book is also for anyone who has to quickly take over a class when the regular teacher unexpectedly departs the classroom or has a sudden absence. It will allow substitute teachers and others to quickly acquire key information that will make the difference between a good day of teaching and a complete disaster.

This book is dedicated to America's teachers. Their job sometimes seems impossible, but they get it done.

A special thanks to
Fran Huber, teaching colleague,
Lasley Elementary School;
Karen Fitzpatrick, principal;
Shannon Kieber, teacher; and
Scotta Williams, teacher.

Contents

The Author   ix

Preface   **xi**

1. Overview of Lesson Plans   1

2. Kindergarten Lesson Plans   9

3. First Grade Lesson Plans   19

4. Second Grade Lesson Plans   39

5. Third Grade Lesson Plans   59

6. Fourth Grade Lesson Plans   81

7. Fifth Grade Lesson Plans   109

8. Overview of Advice   147

9. Advice to the Regular Teacher   149

10. Advice to the Substitute Teacher   155

Epilogue   **163**

The Author

John Dellinger taught in the public school systems of Riverside, California; Boulder, Colorado; Steamboat Springs, Colorado; and Denver, Colorado. After retiring from the Denver Public Schools, he continued to teach as a substitute in Denver and neighboring Jefferson County.

He is the author of two detective/mystery novels, *Dinosaur Tracks & Murder* and *Homecoming to Murder,* published as audio books by Books in Motion. He has had articles published in the following magazines: *Vietnam, Grit, Wild West, Adventure West, World War II, Military History, Short Stuff, Historically Jeffco, The Retired Officer, Rocky Mountain Rider, Great Battles,* and as part of "Soundings" in *Air & Space/Smithsonian.*

The Substitute Teaching Survival Guide, Grades 6–12: Emergency Lesson Plans and Essential Advice was published in 2005. The successful publication of that book led to the publishing of this book: *The Substitute Teaching Survival Guide, Grades K–5: Emergency Lesson Plans and Essential Advice.*

He holds degrees from two universities: a B.A. from the University of Northern Colorado and an M.A. from the University of Colorado.

Preface

As the title suggests, this book consists of two parts: lesson plans and advice. The greater part of the book is made up of lesson plans, with advice having a smaller role. I have structured the book this way because I feel that most people who find themselves in front of an elementary classroom have at least a fair idea of what is expected of them.

This is not to say that it is easy. Teaching is rarely easy, no matter what the grade level. Little kids may throw up on each other, but they are unlikely to challenge your authority by ignoring your request to stay out of a particular area of the school. Pregnancies are unlikely to occur before a child reaches middle school.

One of my most grateful students was a mother-to-be. I had arranged for her to take the final exam a week ahead of time; thus, she didn't have to worry about coming to class on her due date. Ah, such compassion! Of course, I didn't want the local paper to carry the headline "Teacher Delivers Baby During Final Exam."

As teachers we often find ourselves in challenging circumstances. It is my hope that this book will be helpful in meeting those challenges.

November 2005

John Dellinger
Lakewood, Colorado

Chapter One

Overview of Lesson Plans

Although this book calls them *emergency lesson plans,* a more precise term might be *emergency learning exercises.* Either way you put it, the learning exercises included in these pages will provide you with a lesson plan on any day you choose to use them or at any time you are in need of a quick lesson plan.

Lesson plan implies a number of prescribed steps that a teacher follows to reach one or more learning objectives. A lesson plan usually has defined times to spend on each part of the lesson. This is totally appropriate for secondary students, and it was the course of action I took in writing *The Substitute Teaching Survival Guide, Grades 6–12: Emergency Lesson Plans and Essential Advice.*

In designing lesson plans for younger children, I have chosen to give you more flexibility. I have not prescribed a set amount of time, although I have aimed at about 15 minutes for each kindergarten exercise and about 30 minutes for each exercise for grades 1 through 5. Take as much time as you want to take. If you like the exercise and it is going well, you may wish to dwell on it for a while. If it is something you can do quickly and don't like, wrap it up and move on to another exercise.

Each exercise can stand on its own without requiring the completion of a previous exercise or information from a previous exercise. Therefore, you can skip any exercise you don't want to do and do the exercises in any order you wish. (I hope, however, that you will see the logic in the order I have provided.) Should you need something for only part of the day, pick what you want to use.

I have provided 24 exercises for each of the 6 grade levels, making a total of 144 exercises for you to use. I suppose you either have to be a fool or a genius to think you can make lesson plans for all core subjects in all grade levels. I consider myself neither a fool nor a genius, so it is fortunate I have an editor who has encouraged me in this endeavor.

The exercises generally fall into 4 categories: English and communication, history and heritage, math, science and the physical world. I have not attempted to ensure an equal distribution for all 4 categories. Once a basic skill level in reading and writing is achieved, the

English and communication category is incorporated into the other 3 categories, because writing and communicating are often required to complete an exercise.

A group of 4 exercises will often be related to a topic. The next 4 may be related to a different topic. Thus, you will sometimes have 4 exercises that are closely related to each other but have little or no relationship with the preceding 4 or the following 4.

If you find a group of exercises you don't like, you may want to skip the entire group. Having 24 exercises for each grade level should give you a wide enough selection to find something you like. You may even decide to use something from a different grade level; I do not claim infallibility in placing all exercises at precisely the grade level where they should be. Of course, I hope that you will find most of the exercises to your liking and use them in a way that will provide you with lesson plans for any grade level should the need arise.

I have included exercises on the Pledge of Allegiance, "The Star-Spangled Banner," and other symbols of our heritage because I think it is important for students to be grounded in the benchmarks of our culture. When students say the pledge, they should know that *indivisible* does not mean *invisible*. I suspect that most regular teachers agree that the symbols of our heritage are important and therefore instruct students about these symbols.

Regular teachers work hard at teaching students whatever they need to and should know. I hope that the fill-in exercises here may add a sliver of knowledge to the vast amount of knowledge each teacher imparts to students.

Knowledge was a key word I kept in mind when constructing these exercises. I want students to learn. It is not enough for a substitute teacher just to entertain. Good substitutes, like good regular teachers, do not merely fill a student's time. They use mental exercises to help students stretch their minds and develop mental strength, just as physical exercises develop muscle tone and body strength.

Some of these exercises may seem too advanced for the grade level in which I have placed them. Should second graders have exercises that teach them how hail is formed and what causes lightning? Should fourth graders be doing math problems where the problems and answers are written in Roman numerals? Should fifth graders be told about the Marshall Plan that gave aid to Western Europe after World War II? In my opinion, yes.

All students are not expected to know or totally understand everything you read to them in the exercises. Some students will understand completely what you say, others will only understand a part of it. What is important is that every student or nearly every student will be able to do what the exercise requires the students to do. When you tell them to copy something, they will be able to copy as instructed. When you have them answer a question or draw a picture, they will be able to do what you ask them to do.

Why do students sometimes seem to know so little? In my humble opinion, one reason is that we sometimes don't expect them to know much. We don't have to go in lockstep, catering to the lowest common denominator. It has been my experience that in the same lesson plan you can give the brighter kids something to chew on and expand their horizons while giving all kids in a "normal" class, regardless of ability, something that interests them and increases their knowledge.

Something that may seem a little unusual to some teachers today is having students copy something from the board rather than putting the information in a handout; often a paper is passed out for students to fill in the blanks or something similar. But if you were required to run off a handout before class, it would defeat the purpose of the lesson plans in this book.

They are ready to use without your even having to look at them or do anything before entering the classroom.

Furthermore, having students copy what you have written on the board teaches writing and helps you maintain control in the classroom. When students are actively copying from the board, they are not free to wander in mind and body. The hand that is moving the pencil is not free to throw a spitball. Copying an *excessive* amount of material, however, is not recommended, because your students will start to complain if there is too much copying at 1 time.

How should these learning exercises be used? If you are substituting and have no lesson plan, use these exercises. If you are an administrator, counselor, or teacher called to take over a class on a minute's notice with no lesson plan, use these exercises. If you are a regular teacher who has to leave the classroom in an emergency with no lesson plan, leave a note: "Do exercises _____ on pages _____." If you are a regular teacher and find a lesson you want to teach, please do. You could do me no greater honor than thinking something I have planned for a lesson is worthy of your use.

The only materials students need to complete any of these exercises are a pencil and paper. Elementary classrooms are usually wonderful for having a wide assortment of materials available (sometimes purchased by the teacher at the teacher's own expense or purchased by parents at the parents' expense). If crayons, glue, construction paper, and so on are available, you may wish to have students make judicious use of them. ("Judicious" because a regular teacher doesn't want to come back to find that a substitute used a month's supply of construction paper in one day.) A bright orange or yellow sun is probably more fun for a student to draw and makes more of an impression on the student than a sun drawn in pencil.

What materials do you as a teacher need? Just this book, that's all. As previously stated, you don't have to duplicate or prepare anything. If you can open this book to a page that has an exercise on it (I'm sure you can), and if you can read (I'm sure you can), you are ready to teach the lesson plans.

Here is a list of the emergency lesson plans offered in this book:

Kindergarten Lesson Plans

Exercise 1: First Letters of Names

Exercise 2: Number of Names with Same First Letter

Exercise 3: Alphabetical Order of Names

Exercise 4: Random Identification of First Letters

Exercise 5: Earth and Sun

Exercise 6: Earth and Moon

Exercise 7: Earth, Moon, Sun (Drawing)

Exercise 8: Earth, Moon, Sun (Physically Rotating)

Exercise 9: Numbers (Writing and Standing)

Exercise 10: Numbers (Naming and Demonstrating)

Exercise 11: Numbers (Counting and Standing)

Exercise 12: Numbers (Writing and Connecting)

Exercise 13: The 24-Hour Day

Exercise 14: Telling Time

Exercise 15: Seconds and Minutes

Exercise 16: Days of the Week

Exercise 17: Months of the Year

Exercise 18: Birthday Months

Exercise 19: Federal Holidays

Exercise 20: Special Days

Exercise 21: Spring

Exercise 22: Summer

Exercise 23: Autumn

Exercise 24: Winter

First Grade Lesson Plans

Exercise 1: Silly Rhymes for A, B, C, D

Exercise 2: Names and Sentences for A, B, C, D

Exercise 3: Silly Rhymes for E, F, G, H

Exercise 4: Names and Sentences for E, F, G, H

Exercise 5: The National Anthem (Memorizing)

Exercise 6: The National Anthem (Printing)

Exercise 7: The American Flag (Drawing)

Exercise 8: The Pledge of Allegiance (Printing and Memorizing)

Exercise 9: Silly Rhymes for I, J, K, L

Exercise 10: Names and Sentences for I, J, K, L

Exercise 11: Silly Rhymes for M, N, O, P

Exercise 12: Names and Sentences for M, N, O, P

Exercise 13: Planets: Position

Exercise 14: Planets: Size

Exercise 15: Planets: Orbits, Temperatures

Exercise 16: Planets: Unique Facts

Exercise 17: Silly Rhymes for Q, R, S, T

Exercise 18: Names and Sentences for Q, R, S, T

Exercise 19: Silly Rhymes for U, V, W, X

Exercise 20: Names and Sentences for U, V, W, X

Exercise 21: Silly Rhymes for Y, Z

Exercise 22: "Yankee Doodle" (Memorizing)

Exercise 23: "Yankee Doodle" (Printing)

Exercise 24: "Yankee Doodle" (Drawing)

Second Grade Lesson Plans

Exercise 1: George Washington

Exercise 2: John Adams

Exercise 3: Thomas Jefferson

Exercise 4: Lewis and Clark

Exercise 5: Standing Math: Addition

Exercise 6: Standing Math: Subtraction

Exercise 7: Standing Math: Multiplication

Exercise 8: Addition, Subtraction, Multiplication

Exercise 9: James Madison

Exercise 10: James Monroe

Exercise 11: John Quincy Adams

Exercise 12: Erie Canal

Exercise 13: Sunshine, Temperature

Exercise 14: Winds, Fronts

Exercise 15: Clouds, Fog

Exercise 16: Dew, Frost, Ice

Exercise 17: Andrew Jackson

Exercise 18: Martin Van Buren

Exercise 19: William Henry Harrison

Exercise 20: Oklahoma

Exercise 21: Rain, Snow, Sleet, Hail

Exercise 22: Lightning, Thunder

Exercise 23: Tornadoes, Hurricanes

Exercise 24: TV Weather Person

Third Grade Lesson Plans

Exercise 1: States 1–13

Exercise 2: States 14–26

Exercise 3: States 27–38

Exercise 4: States 39–50

Exercise 5: John Tyler

Exercise 6: James Knox Polk

Exercise 7: Zachary Taylor

Exercise 8: Texas

Exercise 9: Money Math: Addition

Exercise 10: Money Math: Subtraction

Exercise 11: Money Math: Multiplication

Exercise 12: Money Math: Addition, Subtraction, Multiplication

Exercise 13: Millard Fillmore

Exercise 14: Franklin Pierce

Exercise 15: James Buchanan

Exercise 16: California

Exercise 17: Water

Exercise 18: Oil

Exercise 19: Natural Gas

Exercise 20: Coal

Exercise 21: Abraham Lincoln

Exercise 22: Andrew Johnson

Exercise 23: Ulysses Simpson Grant

Exercise 24: Gettysburg

Fourth Grade Lesson Plans

Exercise 1: Flowers

Exercise 2: Trees

Exercise 3: Fish

Exercise 4: Birds

Exercise 5: Rutherford B. Hayes

Exercise 6: James Garfield and Chester Alan Arthur

Exercise 7: Grover Cleveland

Exercise 8: Benjamin Harrison

Exercise 9: Roman Numerals: I–XXX

Exercise 10: Roman Numerals: Converting to Arabic

Exercise 11: Roman Numerals: Addition

Exercise 12: Roman Numerals: Subtraction

Exercise 13: William McKinley

Exercise 14: Theodore Roosevelt

Exercise 15: William Howard Taft

Exercise 16: Woodrow Wilson

Exercise 17: "America" ("My Country 'Tis of Thee")

Exercise 18: "America the Beautiful"

Exercise 19: Army Song and Air Force Song

Exercise 20: Navy Song, Marine Song, Coast Guard Song

Exercise 21: Warren Harding

Exercise 22: Calvin Coolidge

Exercise 23: Herbert Hoover

Exercise 24: Franklin D. Roosevelt

Fifth Grade Lesson Plans

Exercise 1: The Heart

Exercise 2: The Lungs

Exercise 3: The Liver

Exercise 4: The Kidneys

Exercise 5: Harry Truman

Exercise 6: Dwight Eisenhower

Exercise 7: John Kennedy

Exercise 8: Lyndon Johnson

Exercise 9: "Paul Revere's Ride"

Exercise 10: "Old Ironsides"

Exercise 11: "The Ship of State"

Exercise 12: "The Flag Goes By"

Exercise 13: Ears

Exercise 14: Eyes

Exercise 15: Teeth

Exercise 16: Skin and Hair

Exercise 17: Richard Nixon

Exercise 18: Gerald Ford

Exercise 19: Jimmy Carter

Exercise 20: Ronald Reagan

Exercise 21: The Statue of Liberty, Mount Rushmore

Exercise 22: George Herbert Walker Bush

Exercise 23: Bill Clinton

Exercise 24: George Walker Bush

Chapter Two

Kindergarten Lesson Plans

Exercise 1: First Letters of Names

1. Have the students say in unison: "A."

2. Have all students whose first names begin with A stand up.

3. Have all of the standing students, one at a time, tell one thing they would like the other students to know about themselves.

4. Have the A students sit down.

5. Go on to B and repeat the process until the class has gone through the alphabet.

Exercise 2: Number of Names with Same First Letter

1. Have all students print A on their papers.

2. Have all students whose first name begins with A stand up.

3. Have the class count in unison with you the number of students standing and write that number beside A. (Example: A 2.)

4. Go on to B and repeat the process until you have gone through the alphabet. For letters where there are no students, have the students place a zero after the letter. (Example: E 0.)

5. Have the students circle the letter that has the most students.

Exercise 3: Alphabetical Order of Names

1. Have all students whose first name begins with A stand up.

2. Alphabetize the A's by placing the students in a line in that order. (Example: Abe, Andy, Angela.)

3. Instruct the A students to remember the order you have placed them in and have them sit down.

4. Go on to B and repeat the process until you have gone through the alphabet.

5. Have all of the students stand up and put themselves in a long alphabetized line.

6. Have the students repeat the alphabet as you walk the line beside them, saying "A," "B," and so on.

Exercise 4: Random Identification of First Letters

1. Choose a student and ask the student his or her name.

 2. Print the first letter of the student's first name on the board and have all students copy the letter.

3. Have the student whose letter you wrote choose another student.

 4. Write the first letter of the second student's first name on the board and have the class copy the letter.

5. Continue the process until all the students have been included.

Exercise 5: Earth and Sun

1. Tell the students they are going to draw 2 circles: the first will be the Sun, the second will be the Earth. Ask them which circle should be bigger.

2. Explain that the Earth revolves around the Sun and that the Sun is bigger but looks small because it is far away.

3. Have the students draw the 2 circles, putting an E next to Earth and an S next to the Sun.

4. Have individual students show their pictures to the class.

Exercise 6: Earth and Moon

1. Tell the students they are going to draw 2 circles; the first will be the Earth and the second will be the Moon. Ask them which circle should be bigger.

2. Explain that the Moon revolves around the Earth and that the Earth is bigger.

3. Have the students draw 2 circles, putting an E next to Earth and an M next to the Moon.

4. Have individual students show their pictures to the class.

Exercise 7: Earth, Moon, Sun (Drawing)

1. Tell the students they are going to draw 3 circles: Earth, Moon, and Sun. Ask them which circle should be the biggest and which circle should be the smallest.

2. Explain that the Moon revolves around the Earth while the Earth is going around the Sun.

3. Have the students draw 3 circles, putting an E next to Earth, an S next to the Sun, and an M next to the Moon.

4. Have individual students show their pictures to the class.

Exercise 8: Earth, Moon, Sun (Physically Rotating)

1. Tell the students that each of them will be a Sun, an Earth, or a Moon. Have the students count off, "Sun, Earth, Moon; Sun, Earth, Moon" until everyone in the class has been labeled.

2. Have all of the Suns go to a corner of the room, the Earths to a different corner, and the Moons to yet another corner.

3. Have each of the Suns choose an Earth and a Moon. If it comes out uneven, send the extra Sun (and maybe Earth) to the fourth corner of the room, telling these children that they are a distant star and its planet.

4. Have the Suns stand stationary while the Earths rotate around the Suns and the Moons rotate around the Earths.

5. When you think the students have done enough rotating (and become silly enough), stop the exercise.

Exercise 9: Numbers (Writing and Standing)

1. Have all students write the number 1 on their papers.

2. Have 1 student stand up and sit down.

3. Have all students write the number 2 on their papers.

4. Have the student who previously stood up stand up again and have another student stand up.

5. Have both students sit down.

6. Repeat the process with 3 and continue on until the entire class has been counted.

Exercise 10: Numbers (Naming and Demonstrating)

1. Divide the class into 2 teams and have them line up on opposite sides of the room, facing each other.

2. Select a student from either team to start the game.

3. Tell the student to call on a member of the other team to step forward and bring out a number of students with her or him. (Example: "I want Shauna to come out with 3 students.") The students return to the line after they have been counted. When a child brings out the correct number of students, that child's team earns a point.

4. Repeat the process, alternating back and forth between teams. Keep score. The team that earns 10 points first wins.

Exercise 11: Numbers (Counting and Standing)

1. Have students count off, "1, 2, 3, 4" and so on, giving each student a different number.

2. Each time you lead the class in counting in unison, tell them what numbers you want to stand up when the numbers are called. (Example: 7 and 10.) As the class counts in unison, the students who have the numbers you designated stand up. When the count is finished, they sit down but will continue to stand up each time the class counts.

3. Repeat the process, adding new numbers each time before the class counts in unison.

4. When all students are standing, you may wish to repeat the process in reverse, having students sit down.

Exercise 12: Numbers (Writing and Connecting)

1. Tell the students to write the number 1 anyplace they want to on their papers. (Encourage some students to write it in the top right corner, others to write it in the middle-bottom, and so on, anywhere they choose.)

2. Have them write 2 anyplace on their papers. Continue the process until they have written the number 10.

3. Have the students draw a line from 1 to 2, then from 2 to 3, and so on up to 10.

4. When all of the numbers have been connected, have the students hold up their papers to see if any of the papers looks like a picture of something.

5. If you so desire, on a new sheet of paper repeat the process using the numbers 11 through 20.

Exercise 13: The 24-Hour Day

1. Ask the students how many hours are in a day.

2. Have the class count in unison from 1 to 24.

3. Have the students write 1 to 12 on their papers as the class counts in unison from 1 to 12.

4. Have the students print A.M. beside each of the numbers.

5. Have the students write 1 to 12 on their papers as the class again counts in unison from 1 to 12.

6. Have the students print P.M. beside each of the numbers.

7. Start with 1 A.M. and ask the class what people are usually doing at that time (sleeping).

8. Go on to 2 A.M. and all 24 hours, eliciting responses from the class on what people might be doing at those times.

Exercise 14: Telling Time

1. Have the students draw a large circle on their papers.

2. Have the students write the numbers 1 to 12 inside the circle, putting 12 at the top and putting the rest of the numbers where they would be on a clock.

3. Have the students put a dot in the middle of the circle and from that dot draw the long hand of the clock up to 12.

4. Tell the students to draw a shorter hand to any other number they choose.

5. Have individual students hold up their clock pictures and let the class figure out what time it is on each clock picture.

6. Have a student stand up, holding his or her clock picture, and then have the student point to another student.

7. Have the student who is pointed to identify the time on the clock by saying "Ticktock, the clock says _____ o'clock."

8. Continue the ticktock game as long as you wish.

Exercise 15: Seconds and Minutes

1. Ask the class: "How many seconds are in a minute?"
2. Have the class say 3 times in unison: "There are 60 seconds in a minute."
3. Ask the class: "How many minutes are in an hour?"
4. Have the class say 3 times in unison: "There are 60 minutes in an hour."
5. Ask the class: "How many seconds are in a minute and how many minutes are in an hour?"
6. Have the class say 3 times in unison: "There are 60 seconds in a minute and 60 minutes in an hour."
7. If there is a functioning clock in the classroom, have students sit quietly and watch the clock as it measures 2 minutes. (If you have no clock, have the students sit quietly while you use a watch to measure 2 minutes.)
8. Have the students put their left index fingers on top of their heads, holding their fingers in place while they sit quietly for 1 minute.
9. Repeat the process as many times as you like, having the children touch their finger to their right ear, left elbow, and so on while you vary the time. (Example: "I want you to touch your right finger to your left elbow for 30 seconds.")

Exercise 16: Days of the Week

1. Ask the class if anybody can recite the days of the week.
2. Have the class say the days of the week 3 times in unison.
3. Have the class count the number of days in the week.
4. Say "Sunday" and have each student print S.
5. Go on to Monday and through the rest of the week having students print the first letter of each day of the week.
6. Have the class identify the days of the week that begin with the same letters.
7. Have each student print S-S to indicate Sunday and Saturday, T-T to indicate Tuesday and Thursday, then M-W-F to indicate Monday, Wednesday, and Friday.

Exercise 17: Months of the Year

1. Ask the class if anybody can recite the months of the year.
2. Have the class say the months of the year 3 times in unison.

3. Have the class count the number of months in the year.

4. Say "January" and have each student print J.

5. Go on to February and through the rest of the year, having each student print the first letter of each month.

6. Have the class identify which months of the year begin with the same letters. Have each student print J-J-J for January, June, July; M-M for March, May; A-A for April, August.

7. Have each student print F-S-O-N-D for February, September, October, November, December.

Exercise 18: Birthday Months

1. Ask the class if anybody has a birthday in January. Have all members of the class print the first letter of that student's first name, J for January, and the day of the student's birthday. (Examples: Heather's birthday is January 5. H-J-5. Paula's birthday is January 12. P-J-12.)

2. Go on to February and repeat the process, continuing through the rest of the year.

Exercise 19: Federal Holidays

1. Tell the class that federal holidays are special days that the government has officially recognized as holidays.

2. Tell the class that they are going to print some letters and numbers for each federal holiday.

3. As you identify each holiday, write the corresponding letters and numbers on the board and have the students copy them:

   (1) NYD-J-1 (for New Year's Day, January 1)

   (2) MLKJD-J-3M (for Martin Luther King Jr. Day, third Monday in January)

   (3) PD-F-3M (for Presidents' Day, third Monday in February)

   (4) MD-M-LM (for Memorial Day, last Monday in May)

   (5) ID-J-4 (for Independence Day, July 4)

   (6) LD-S-1M (for Labor Day, first Monday in September)

   (7) CD-O-2M (for Columbus Day, second Monday in October)

   (8) VD-N-11 (for Veterans Day, November 11)

   (9) TD-N-4T (for Thanksgiving Day, fourth Thursday in November)

   (10) CD-D-25 (for Christmas Day, December 25)

Exercise 20: Special Days

1. Tell the class that there are special days that some people celebrate.

2. Tell the class that they are going to print letters and numbers for each special day you tell them about.

 3. As you identify each holiday, write the corresponding letters and numbers on the board and have the students copy them:

   (1) GD-F-2 (for Groundhog Day, February 2; groundhog does or doesn't show its shadow)

   (2) VD-F-14 (for Valentine's Day, February 14)

   (3) SPD-M-17 (for St. Patrick's Day, March 17)

   (4) AFD-A-1 (for April Fool's Day, April 1)

   (5) AD-A-LF (for Arbor Day, usually the last Friday in April; day for planting trees)

   (6) CD-M-5 (for Cinco de Mayo, May 5)

   (7) MD-M-2S (for Mother's Day, second Sunday in May)

   (8) FD-J-14 (for Flag Day, June 14)

   (9) FD-J-3S (for Father's Day, third Sunday in June)

   (10) GD-S-SALD (for Grandparents' Day, first Sunday after Labor Day)

Exercise 21: Spring

1. Tell the students there are 4 seasons in the year: spring, summer, autumn (fall), and winter.

2. Have them print S for spring, S for summer, A for autumn, and W for winter.

3. Tell them spring begins for the northern half of the world (Northern Hemisphere) on March 20 and lasts until summer begins on June 21.

4. Have them print M-20 for March 20.

5. Tell them that spring is the time when flowers begin to come up and trees start to get leaves.

6. Have each student draw a picture showing flowers beginning to sprout and a tree that is starting to get leaves.

7. Have students show their pictures to the class.

Exercise 22: Summer

1. Tell the students there are 4 seasons in the year: spring, summer, autumn (fall), and winter.
2. Have them print S for spring, S for summer, A for autumn, and W for winter.
3. Tell them summer begins for the northern half of the world (Northern Hemisphere) on June 21 and lasts until autumn begins on September 22.
4. Have them print J-21 for June 21.
5. Tell them summer is the time when flowers are in full bloom and a tree has lots of full-grown leaves.
6. Have each student draw a picture showing flowers in full bloom and a tree with lots of full-grown leaves.
7. Have students show their pictures to the class.

Exercise 23: Autumn

1. Tell the students there are 4 seasons in the year: spring, summer, autumn (fall), and winter.
2. Have them print S for spring, S for summer, A for autumn, and W for winter.
3. Tell them autumn begins for the northern half of the world (Northern Hemisphere) on September 22 and lasts until winter begins on December 21.
4. Have them print S-22 for September 22.
5. Tell them autumn is the time of year when flowers begin to die and trees start dropping their leaves.
6. Have each student draw a picture showing flowers dying and a tree that is dropping leaves.
7. Have students show their pictures to the class.

Exercise 24: Winter

1. Tell the students there are 4 seasons in the year: spring, summer, autumn (fall), and winter.
2. Have them print S for spring, S for summer, A for autumn, and W for winter.

3. Tell them winter begins for the northern half of the world (Northern Hemisphere) on December 21 and lasts until spring begins on March 20.

4. Have them print D-21 for December 21.

5. Tell them winter is the time of year when the flowers are gone and the trees have no leaves.

6. Have each student draw a picture where there are no flowers, there is a tree that has no leaves, and it looks like winter.

7. Have students show their pictures to the class.

Chapter Three

First Grade Lesson Plans

Exercise 1: Silly Rhymes for A, B, C, D

Read Aloud)))   1. Read to the class:

Alissa Antelope ran very fast.
She never ended up last.
Her time she never took.
She fell down because she forgot to look.

2. Have the students print "Alissa Antelope."

Read Aloud)))   3. Read to the class:

Bartram Bird was a terrible flier
And also a terrible liar.
When he met his friends at the birdbath,
He made up stories that his flying was great.
But they knew the truth, because he was always late.

4. Have the students print "Bartram Bird."

Read Aloud)))   5. Read to the class:

Clarissa Clam didn't want to become a clam cake,
So she disguised herself as a fish.
But she still ended up on a dish.

6. Have the students print "Clarissa Clam."

7. Read to the class:

Delbert Dog thought he was a hog.
He rolled in the mud so much,
His tail curled up in a Q,
And he smelled P.U.

8. Have the students print "Delbert Dog."

9. Have each student choose one of the rhymes and draw a picture of it, printing the appropriate name on the picture: "Alissa Antelope," "Bartram Bird," "Clarissa Clam," or "Delbert Dog."

10. Have all students who drew Alissa Antelope stand up as a group and show the class their pictures. Do the same with the other three groups.

Exercise 2: Names and Sentences for A, B, C, D

1. Read to the class: "Abigail Adams was the wife of President John Adams."

2. Have the students print "Abigail Adams."

3. Read to the class: "Buffalo Bill got his name by hunting buffalo."

4. Have the students print "Buffalo Bill."

5. Read to the class: "Charlie Chaplin was a star in silent movies."

6. Have the students print "Charlie Chaplin."

7. Read to the class: "Donald Duck was in a lot of cartoons and comics."

8. Have the students print "Donald Duck."

9. Say to the class: "I am going to read aloud the names of 4 things or people and you are going to tell me which of the 4 names you just wrote down goes with each of them. Then we are going to print the things that go together."

    Walt Disney

    Have students print "Donald Duck, Walt Disney."

    Horse

    Have students print "Buffalo Bill, horse."

    Hollywood

    Have students print "Charlie Chaplin, Hollywood."

    First Lady

    Have students print "Abigail Adams, First Lady."

10. Have students print the following sentences:

Alice ate an apple.

Big bugs bit Betty.

Carl caught cold.

Dan drove downtown.

Exercise 3: Silly Rhymes for E, F, G, H

Read Aloud))) 1. Read to the class:

Esther Elephant went to a dance
In hopes of finding romance.
There was just one other elephant there,
But he just didn't seem to care
Until they danced and she stepped on his toe.

2. Have students print "Esther Elephant."

Read Aloud))) 3. Read to the class:

Francis Frog sat on a log
Croaking away all day.
She thought she was a singing star,
But no one came from near or far.

4. Have students print "Francis Frog."

Read Aloud))) 5. Read to the class:

Gloster Goat ate a coat,
Then he began to bloat.
He decided the next time he would dine,
A sweater would do just fine.

6. Have students print "Gloster Goat."

Read Aloud))) 7. Read to the class:

Holly Hippopotamus soaked in water
To keep from getting hotter.
Stuck in the mud when the water drained,
She was very happy when it rained.

8. Have students print "Holly Hippopotamus."

9. Have each student choose one of the rhymes and draw a picture of it, printing the appropriate name on the picture: "Esther Elephant," "Francis Frog," "Gloster Goat," or "Holly Hippopotamus."

10. Have all students who drew Esther Elephant stand up as a group to show the class their pictures. Do the same with the other 3 groups.

Exercise 4: Names and Sentences for E, F, G, H

 Read Aloud
1. Read to the class: "Edward Elgar composed the music 'Pomp and Circumstance.'"

2. Have the students print "Edward Elgar."

 Read Aloud
3. Read to the class: "Felix Frankfurter was a judge on the Supreme Court."

4. Have students print "Felix Frankfurter."

Read Aloud
5. Read to the class: "Galileo Galilei used a telescope to see things in the sky."

6. Have the students print "Galileo Galilei."

Read Aloud
7. Read to the class: "Henry Heinz started a business to put food in cans, bottles, and packages."

8. Have the students print "Henry Heinz."

9. Say to the class: "I am going to read aloud the names of 4 things, and you are going to tell me which of the 4 names you just wrote goes with each of them. Then we are going to print the things that go together."

ketchup (catsup)

Have students print "Henry Heinz, ketchup."

black robe

Have students print "Felix Frankfurter, black robe."

orchestra

Have students print "Edward Elgar, orchestra."

planet

Have students print "Galileo Galilei, planet."

 Write on Board
10. Have students print the following sentences:

Elroy eats eggs.

Frank forgot.

George gets good grades.

Harriet hurried home.

Exercise 5: The National Anthem (Memorizing)

1. Say to the class: "Countries have a special song that they call the national anthem. Our national anthem is 'The Star-Spangled Banner.' You hear it a lot. We are going to memorize some of the words so that you will know what they are. We are going to memorize 8 lines, so I am going to divide you into 8 groups and have each group memorize a line."

2. Divide the class into 8 groups according to where they are sitting, numbering each group.

 3. Print this first line on the board:

(1) Oh, say can you see by the dawn's early light,

4. You say the line.

5. Have the entire class say the line in unison.

6. Have the first group say the line in unison.

7. Tell the group that they are to remember the line.

8. Erase the line.

 9. Repeat this process with each of the following lines, using a different group with each line: Write the line on the board. Read it aloud. Have the entire class repeat it. Have a group repeat it. Erase the line, and go on to the next.

(2) What so proudly we hailed at the twilight's last gleaming?

(3) Whose broad stripes and bright stars, through the perilous fight,

(4) O'er the ramparts we watched, were so gallantly streaming!

(5) And the rockets' red glare, the bombs bursting in air,

(6) Gave proof through the night that our flag was still there.

(7) Oh, say does that star-spangled banner yet wave

(8) O'er the land of the free and the home of the brave?

10. Have each group of children repeat their line from memory, putting the entire stanza together; then have the entire class say the entire stanza in unison.

Exercise 6: The National Anthem (Printing)

1. Print "The Star-Spangled Banner" on the board and have the class copy it. (Their printing skills will be limited, so it may take quite a while for them to complete the task.)

   (1) Oh, say can you see by the dawn's early light,

   (2) What so proudly we hailed at the twilight's last gleaming?

   (3) Whose broad stripes and bright stars, through the perilous fight,

   (4) O'er the ramparts we watched, were so gallantly streaming!

   (5) And the rockets' red glare, the bombs bursting in air,

   (6) Gave proof through the night that our flag was still there.

   (7) Oh, say does that star-spangled banner yet wave

   (8) O'er the land of the free and the home of the brave?

2. While some students are still finishing, have students who have already finished stand and try to recite the words from memory without looking at the board.

Exercise 7: The American Flag (Drawing)

1. Have students draw an American flag:

   Make 13 stripes (if in color, make the top stripe red and then every other stripe red).

   Put 13 stars in a circle to represent the original 13 states rather than having students try to do 50 stars.

2. Have students show their completed pictures to the class.

Exercise 8: The Pledge of Allegiance (Printing and Memorizing)

1. Print the Pledge of Allegiance on the board and have the students copy it (their printing skills will be limited, so it may take quite a while for them to complete the task):

I pledge allegiance to the flag of the United States of America and to the republic for which it stands, one nation (under God), indivisible, with liberty and justice for all.

2. Explain to the class:

"Pledge allegiance" means to promise loyalty (support, respect, honor) to the flag, to think of the flag as something special.

"Republic" means a country where people are elected by votes of the people to represent the people.

"Indivisible" means our country cannot be divided (split up) into parts.

"Liberty" means freedom.

"Justice" means treating people fairly.

3. Have individual students who volunteer stand and recite the pledge from memory without looking at the board.

Exercise 9: Silly Rhymes for I, J, K, L

 Read Aloud 1. Read to the class:

Isador Iguana wished he could fly high
To catch a fly.
Instead, he flicked his tongue out.
But the fly was no longer about,
So Isador started to cry about the fly
That flew so high and went bye-bye.

2. Have students print "Isador Iguana."

Read Aloud 3. Read to the class:

Jacqueline Jackal made a mournful sound,
So sad was she that no one was around.
From the other jackals, she got lost.
When she tried to join the hyenas, she got tossed.
Poor Jacqueline, alone in the world at night.
She knew things would get better at daylight.

4. Have students print "Jacqueline Jackal."

Read Aloud 5. Read to the class:

Kenneth Kangaroo went to the Olympics to box.
He knocked the other boxers out of their socks.
When they tried to give him a gold medal on a special day,
He just laughed and hopped away.

6. Have students print "Kenneth Kangaroo."

7. Read to the class:

Lillian Leopard challenged Charlene Cheetah to a race.
Lillian tried so hard, she fell on her face.
Charlene helped her up and told her it was no disgrace.
If you lose when you try,
There is no need to cry.

8. Have students print "Lillian Leopard."

9. Have each student choose 1 of the rhymes and draw a picture of it, printing the appropriate name on the picture: "Isador Iguana," "Jacqueline Jackal," "Kenneth Kangaroo," or "Lillian Leopard."

10. Have all students who drew Isador Iguana stand up as a group to show the class their pictures. Do the same with the other 3 groups.

Exercise 10: Names and Sentences for I, J, K, L

1. Read to the class: "Isabella was a famous queen."

2. Have students print "Isabella."

3. Read to the class: "James Joyce was a famous writer."

4. Have students print "James Joyce."

5. Read to the class: "Kublai Khan was visited by Marco Polo."

6. Have students print "Kublai Khan."

7. Read to the class: "Lennox Lewis was a heavyweight boxing champion."

8. Have students print "Lennox Lewis."

9. Say to the class: "I am going to read aloud the names of 4 things or people, and you are going to tell me which of the 4 names you just wrote goes with each of them. Then we are going to print the things that go together."

   ring

   Have students print "Lennox Lewis, ring."

   China

   Have students print "Kublai Khan, China."

   books

   Have students print "James Joyce, books."

   Columbus

   Have students print "Isabella, Columbus."

10. Have students print the following sentences:

It is invisible.

Jim jabbed Jerry.

Kindergarten kids kiss kittens.

Lucy liked lollipops.

Exercise 11: Silly Rhymes for M, N, O, P

 1. Read to the class:

Matilda Monkey liked to hang by her tail,
Until a wind came up in a strong gale.
It spun her around time and time again
So fast around the branch again and again,
It wrapped her up like a ball of string
So tight she could not even sing.

2. Have students print "Matilda Monkey."

 3. Read to the class:

Natalie Newfoundland was a Canadian dog
Who got to chasing a frog.
The frog hopped away as fast as it could
Into a pond by a wood.
Natalie splashed into the water as fast as she could
Without even wondering if she should.
The frog got away
And Natalie was shivering all day.

4. Have students print "Natalie Newfoundland."

 5. Read to the class:

Oscar Owl liked to hoot.
If he had a horn he would have given a toot.
With such big eyes and otherwise a quiet bird,
You wonder why he wanted to be heard.

6. Have students print "Oscar Owl."

7. Read to the class:

Priscilla Porcupine had sharp needles to spare,
They came right out of her hair.
Why they were there
Was to tell everyone: Beware!

8. Have students print "Priscilla Porcupine."

9. Have each student choose 1 of the rhymes and draw a picture of it, printing the appropriate name on the picture: "Matilda Monkey," "Natalie Newfoundland," "Oscar Owl," or "Priscilla Porcupine."

10. Have all students who drew Matilda Monkey stand up as a group to show the class their pictures. Do the same with the other 3 groups.

Exercise 12: Names and Sentences for M, N, O, P

 1. Read the following sentences to the class: "Mickey Mantle was a famous baseball player."

2. Have students print "Mickey Mantle."

 3. Read to the class: "Nefertiti was a queen."

4. Have students print "Nefertiti."

5. Read to the class: "Osceola was a tribal leader of the Seminoles."

6. Have students print "Osceola."

7. Read to the class: "Pablo Picasso was a famous artist."

8. Have students print "Pablo Picasso."

9. Say to the class, "I am going to read aloud the names of 4 things, and you are going to tell me which of the 4 names you just wrote goes with each of them. Then we are going to print the things that go together."

painting

Have students print "Pablo Picasso, painting."

Egypt

Have students print "Nefertiti, Egypt."

home run

Have students print "Mickey Mantle, home run."

Native American

Have students print "Osceola, Native American."

10. Have students print the following sentences:

Melinda makes magnificent macaroons.

Nobody noticed Norman.

Oliver occasionally obeyed.

Paul painted pictures.

Exercise 13: Planets: Position

1. Say to the class: "Our Earth is a planet and it goes around the Sun. There are other planets that revolve around the Sun. Mercury is the closest planet to the Sun so we are going to print its name first."

2. Have students print the names of the planets, in order of their distance from the sun, as follows:

   (1) Mercury

   (2) Venus

   (3) Earth

   (4) Mars

   (5) Jupiter

   (6) Saturn

   (7) Uranus

   (8) Neptune

   (9) Pluto

3. Explain to the students that although Pluto is usually farther from the Sun than Neptune is, sometimes Pluto is closer.

4. On a new sheet of paper have students draw a circle in the center of the page to represent the Sun, making it about the size of a golf ball. Place nine dots around the Sun to represent the planets. Label each dot with the name of a planet, with Mercury being the closest dot to the Sun and Pluto being the dot that is farthest away.

Exercise 14: Planets: Size

1. Have students copy the following:

Planets (in order of closeness to the Sun)	Size (mass)
Mercury	8
Venus	6
Earth	5
Mars	7
Jupiter	1
Saturn	2
Uranus	4
Neptune	3
Pluto	9

2. On a new sheet of paper have students draw a circle in the center of the page to represent the Sun, making it about the size of a golf ball. Place nine dots around the Sun to represent the planets, leaving enough room to make circles around the dots with the biggest circle being labeled "Jupiter," which should be about the size of a quarter. (Proportions will not be to exact scale; you are merely trying to give students a rough idea of the size of planets in relationship to each other.) Have students reduce the size of each planet until they finally label Pluto, which should remain a mere dot.

Exercise 15: Planets: Orbits, Temperatures

1. Explain to the class that it takes Earth 365 days to go around (orbit) the Sun, and that this amount of time is what we call a year.

2. Explain to the class that the average daytime temperature on Earth is 59 degrees Fahrenheit.

3. Write this on the board and have the students copy the following (all days are Earth days and temperatures are in Fahrenheit [Source: *The World Almanac and Book of Facts*, 2005]):

Planet	Orbit	Average Daytime Temperature
Mercury	88 days	845
Venus	225 days	867
Earth	365 days	59
Mars	687 days	−24
Jupiter	12 years	−162
Saturn	29 years	−218
Uranus	84 years	−323
Neptune	165 years	−330
Pluto	248 years	−369

Exercise 16: Planets: Unique Facts

1. Tell the class they are going to draw silly planet pictures. Each student will choose a planet and then draw a picture that shows that planet's silliness. They will print the name of the planet on the picture.

2. Read the following to the students:

(1) Mercury has daytime temperatures that reach over 800 degrees Fahrenheit and nighttime temperatures that fall below −300 degrees Fahrenheit.

(2) Venus in its orbit comes closer to Earth than any other planet does.

(3) Earth looks blue when seen by astronauts in space.

(4) Mars has a mountain 15 miles high.

(5) Jupiter has at least 61 moons.

(6) Saturn looks as if it has a bunch of rings around it.

(7) On Uranus the Sun shines continuously for 42 Earth years, and then it is dark for 42 Earth years before the Sun comes out again.

(8) Neptune has winds that travel over 1,300 miles per hour.

(9) The planet Pluto has the same name as the Disneyland dog Pluto.

3. After the students have drawn their pictures, have the students who drew Mercury show their pictures to the class as a group. Then go on to Venus and do the same. Continue with all of the planets.

Exercise 17: Silly Rhymes for Q, R, S, T

1. Read to the class:

Quincy Quarterhorse liked to race
Around the track he ran at an astounding pace.
He won the race and continued to run
For Quincy was not done.
The jockey kept yelling, "Stop!"
Quincy bucked him to the ground in a big flop.
Quincy ran away
And kept running all day.

2. Have students print "Quincy Quarterhorse."

3. Read to the class:

Rhonda Rhinoceros put on her makeup
The minute she would wake up.
She thought it was her duty
Because she knew she was a real beauty.

4. Have students print "Rhonda Rhinoceros."

Read Aloud)))

5. Read to the class:

Samantha Snake liked to bake.
In the sun she could not stay awake.
She forgot to put on her tanning lotion
Then she went to sleep in the sun all day
And she melted away.

6. Have students print "Samantha Snake."

Read Aloud)))

7. Read to the class:

Tommy Tomcat liked to go out at night and prowl
With his cat friends he put up quite a howl
Until Mrs. Olsen snapped him with a wet towel
And he ran away with a different howl.

8. Have students print "Tommy Tomcat."

9. Have each student choose 1 of the rhymes and draw a picture of it, printing the appropriate name on the picture: "Quincy Quarterhorse," "Rhonda Rhinoceros," "Samantha Snake," or "Tommy Tomcat."

10. Have all students who drew Quincy Quarterhorse stand up as a group and show the class their pictures. Do the same with the other 3 groups.

Exercise 18: Names and Sentences for Q, R, S, T

Read Aloud)))

1. Read to the class: "Quetzalcoatl was important to Aztec religion."

2. Have students print "Quetzalcoatl."

Read Aloud)))

3. Read to the class: "Roy Rogers was a movie and TV cowboy."

4. Have students print "Roy Rogers."

Read Aloud)))

5. Read to the class: "Sequoya was a Cherokee Native American."

6. Have students print "Sequoya."

Read Aloud)))

7. Read to the class: "Ted Turner started a TV news station."

8. Have students print "Ted Turner."

9. Say to the class, "I am going to read aloud the names of 4 things and you are going to tell me which of the 4 names you just wrote goes with each of them. Then we are going to print the things that go together."

horse

Have students print "Roy Rogers, horse."

trees

Have students print "Sequoya, trees."

CNN

Have students print "Ted Turner, CNN."

Mexico

Have students print "Quetzalcoatl, Mexico."

10. Have students print the following sentences:

Quenton quit quickly.

Rachel raced Robert.

Sarah sat still.

Teddy talked to Troy.

Exercise 19: Silly Rhymes for U, V, W, X

Read Aloud))) 1. Read to the class:

Ursula Umbrella Bird must be smart and brainy
Living in the tropics where it is hot and rainy.
On her head she has a large tuft of black hair that sticks up and out,
It drains the rain off when she flies about.

2. Have students print "Ursula Umbrella Bird."

Read Aloud))) 3. Read to the class:

Vernon Vulture and his vulture friends circle in the air
Hoping to get a meal from somewhere.
They are not so obscene that they should not be seen,
They are helping to keep the Earth clean.

4. Have students print "Vernon Vulture."

Read Aloud))) 5. Read to the class:

Wilma Whale slips through the water with charm and grace
For her the ocean is the only place.
When she came up to the beach it was not good,
People cared for her and helped her back into the water as soon as they could.

6. Have students print "Wilma Whale."

Read Aloud))) 7. Read to the class:

Xavier Ox pulled a wagon west.
Each day he did his best.
Got the settlers to Oregon 1 day,
Then he sneaked off and ran away,
Because he wanted time to play.

8. Have students print "Xavier Ox."

9. Have each student choose 1 of the rhymes and draw a picture of it, printing the name on the picture: "Ursula Umbrella Bird," "Vernon Vulture," "Wilma Whale," or "Xavier Ox."

10. Have all students who drew Ursula Umbrella Bird stand up as a group to show the class their pictures. Do the same with the other 3 groups.

Exercise 20: Names and Sentences for U, V, W, X

 Read Aloud

1. Read to the class: "'Urban' has been the name of a number of popes."

2. Have students print "Urban."

Read Aloud

3. Read to the class: "Vincent van Gogh was a famous painter."

4. Have students print "Vincent van Gogh."

Read Aloud

5. Read to the class: "Walt Whitman was a famous poet."

6. Have students print "Walt Whitman."

Read Aloud

7. Read to the class: "Xerxes was a king of Persia."

8. Have students print "Xerxes."

9. Say to the class, "I am going to read aloud 4 things and you are going to tell me which of the 4 names you just wrote goes with each of them. Then we are going to print the things that go together."

picture

Have students print "Vincent van Gogh, picture."

poem

Have students print "Walt Whitman, poem."

Vatican

Have students print "Urban, Vatican."

crown

Have students print "Xerxes, crown."

Write on Board

10. Have students print the following sentences:

Ulibari umpired.

Virginia vanished.

Wiley went west.

Xenia x-rayed Xavier.

Exercise 21: Silly Rhymes for Y, Z

 Read Aloud

1. Read to the class:

Yolanda Yak could carry a lot on her back.
She didn't like it when her owner gave her a whack.

She dumped her load of grain bags right there
And told her owner to carry his own fare.
Then she ran away as fast as a hare.

2. Have students print "Yolanda Yak."

3. Read to the class:

Zeb Zebra thought his stripes were wonderful and fine
He thought he was better than donkeys who didn't have a single line.
But when Zeb rolled in the mud his stripes disappeared,
And he realized that everyone was fine
No matter how they appeared.

4. Have students print "Zeb Zebra."

5. Have students print the following sentences:

Yesterday you yelled.

Zelda zigzagged.

6. Have each student choose either Yolanda Yak or Zeb Zebra and draw a picture, printing the appropriate name on the picture: "Yolanda Yak" or "Zeb Zebra."

7. Have students who drew Yolanda Yak stand up as a group and show the class their pictures. Do the same with those who drew Zeb Zebra.

Exercise 22: "Yankee Doodle" (Memorizing)

1. Say to the class: "The song 'Yankee Doodle' was 1 of the first songs to become popular in our country. It became popular more than 200 years ago when Americans fought the British to make ourselves free of their rule. People still sing 'Yankee Doodle' today. We are going to memorize some of the words so that you know what they are. We are going to memorize 8 lines, so I am going to divide you into 8 groups and have each group remember a line."

2. Divide the class into 8 groups according to where they are sitting, numbering each group. Print the first line on the board:

(1) Yankee Doodle went to town,

3. Say the line.
4. Have the entire class say the line in unison.
5. Have the first group say the line in unison.
6. Tell the group to remember the line.
7. Erase the line.

8. Repeat the process with all the other lines: Write the line on the board. Say it. Have the entire class say it. Have a group say it. Erase the line.

> (2) A-ridin' on a pony,
>
> (3) Stuck a feather in his cap
>
> (4) And called it macaroni.
>
> (5) Yankee Doodle, keep it up,
>
> (6) Yankee Doodle Dandy,
>
> (7) Mind the music and the step
>
> (8) And with the girls be handy.

9. Have each group repeat their line from memory, putting all 8 lines together. Then have the class say all 8 lines in unison.

Exercise 23: "Yankee Doodle" (Printing)

 1. Print "Yankee Doodle" on the board and have the class copy it. Their printing skills will be limited, so it may take quite a while for them to complete the task.

> (1) Yankee doodle went to town,
>
> (2) A-ridin' on a pony.
>
> (3) Stuck a feather in his cap
>
> (4) And called it macaroni.
>
> (5) Yankee Doodle, keep it up,
>
> (6) Yankee Doodle Dandy,
>
> (7) Mind the music and the step
>
> (8) And with the girls be handy.

2. While some students are finishing up, have those who have finished writing stand and try to recite the words from memory without looking at the board.

Exercise 24: "Yankee Doodle" (Drawing)

Read Aloud)))   1. Read the words to "Yankee Doodle" to the class:

Yankee Doodle went to town,
A-ridin' on a pony,
Stuck a feather in his cap
And called it macaroni.
Yankee Doodle, keep it up,
Yankee Doodle Dandy,
Mind the music and the step
And with the girls be handy.

2. Tell the class: "There are other verses to 'Yankee Doodle' that are not often heard. Some of these verses were probably added during the war we fought to make ourselves free. These verses tell what a young boy saw when he watched soldiers under the command of George Washington. After going through a number of things that the boy saw, the song finishes up with the following lines." Read them to the class:

I can't tell you half I saw,
They kept up such a smother,
So I took my hat off, made a bow
And scampered home to mother.
Yankee Doodle is the tune
Americans delight in,
'Twill do to whistle, sing or play
And just the thing for fightin'.

3. Have students draw a picture of Yankee Doodle.
4. Have students show their pictures to the class.

Chapter Four

Second Grade Lesson Plans

Exercise 1: George Washington

Read Aloud))) 1. Read to the class:

George Washington was our first president. When he was a boy, he wrote down 110 rules for good behavior. He tried to follow these 110 rules all his life. He loved music and enjoyed playing the flute. He is sometimes called the "Father of Our Country." Our country used to belong to another country called England. Then we fought a war to make ourselves free. It was called the Revolutionary War. George Washington led the American soldiers who fought in the war. After we won the war, he led the group of men who decided what our government should be like. That means they decided who should make rules for our country and how our leaders should be chosen. What they decided is called the Constitution. The Constitution gave Americans the right to choose their top leader, the president. George Washington was chosen president for 4 years. Then he was chosen for another 4 years. People liked him so much that no one would run against him. He was the only president to receive all the votes. He could have been chosen again, but after being president for 8 years, he was tired and wanted to go home to his wife, Martha. The city of Washington, D.C., and the state of Washington were named after him. You can see his picture on dollar bills, and there is a monument to him in Washington, D.C.

2. Have students copy the following:

George Washington (1732–1799)

Leader of American soldiers in the Revolutionary War

In charge when the Constitution was written

First president (1789–1797)

Sometimes called the "Father of Our Country"

3. Tell the class that you want them to think for 2 minutes and you want each of them to come up with 2 things they should do for good behavior.

4. Compile on the board a list of good behavior. Have students copy the list or draw a picture about George Washington or do both.

Exercise 2: John Adams

1. Read to the class:

John Adams was our second president. He was the first president to live in what is now called the "White House." Shortly before his wife, Abigail, joined him at the "President's House," he wrote her: "I pray heaven to bestow the best of blessings on this house and all that shall hereafter inhabit. May none but honest and wise men ever rule under this roof." Fourteen years later, during a war, the President's House was badly burned. When it was rebuilt, it was painted white. Then it became known as the "White House." Before John Adams became president, he had been George Washington's vice president. Before that, he had been America's representative to France, the Netherlands, and England. Before that, he was on the committee that was given the job of writing the Declaration of Independence. The Declaration told England that we wanted to be a separate country. Abigail must have thought that John was away from home a lot. There were no telephones and no e-mail in those days, so they wrote many letters to each other. The letters show that they loved each other and missed each other very much when they were apart.

2. Have students copy the following:

John Adams (1735–1826)

On committee to write the Declaration of Independence

Ambassador to foreign countries

George Washington's vice president

Second president (1797–1801)

3. Tell the class that you want them to think for 2 minutes about what kind of person they think should be in the White House.

4. Compile and write on the board a list of "Good Qualities of a President." Have students copy the list or draw a picture about John Adams or do both.

Exercise 3: Thomas Jefferson

Read Aloud

1. Read to the class:

Before the Declaration of Independence, America was part of a country called England. The Declaration of Independence was written by Thomas Jefferson. It said that we would no longer be a part of England and that we were going to be our own country. England did not want to let us go, so George Washington led American soldiers against England in the Revolutionary War. We won and became the country of the United States of America. After George Washington and John Adams had been president, Thomas Jefferson became president. France wanted to sell the United States a large piece of land called Louisiana. President Jefferson agreed to buy it in what was called the Louisiana Purchase. He then sent a group of men led by Meriwether Lewis and William Clark to explore the new land. The team of explorers was called the Lewis and Clark Expedition. Thomas Jefferson could speak many different languages, and he liked to read the many books he owned. He liked to invent and design things. When George Washington and John Adams were president, people bowed to them. When Thomas Jefferson was president, he let people shake his hand instead. Thomas Jefferson died on July 4, 1826, on the fiftieth anniversary of the signing of the Declaration of Independence.

Write on Board

2. Have students copy the following:

Thomas Jefferson (1743–1826)

Wrote the Declaration of Independence

Third president (1801–1809)

Louisiana Purchase (1803)

Lewis and Clark Expedition (1804–1806)

3. Tell the class to think for 2 minutes about if they would have wanted to go on the Lewis and Clark Expedition if they had been alive back then.

Write on Board

4. Compile on the board 2 columns: "Yes," reasons for going. "No," reasons for not going. Have the students copy the lists on the board or draw a picture of Thomas Jefferson or do both.

Exercise 4: Lewis and Clark

Read Aloud)))

1. Read to the class:

If you go across the country today, you probably will travel by airplane, automobile, train, or bus. It will take you a few hours by airplane and probably a couple of days or so by car, train, or bus. Long ago it took much longer. Meriwether Lewis and William Clark left St. Louis in May 1804 with an exploring expedition of about 40 men. They went by boat, and it took them a year and a half to reach the Pacific Ocean. Before there were roads, rivers were used like highways. Lewis and Clark took their exploring party up the Missouri River. They started for the Pacific in a big boat and 2 little boats. In some places, the river had waterfalls. Then they had to carry the boats around the falling water. In the high mountains, the river became smaller and smaller. There wasn't enough water for their boats, so they left their boats and walked. Fortunately, they obtained horses from helpful Shoshone American Indians. These Indians were related to the Shoshone woman Sacagawea. She had joined the expedition as an interpreter and guide. The expedition made the difficult journey across the mountains and then made canoes from trees. With their canoes, they sailed down the Columbia River. Finally, they reached the Pacific Ocean. They stayed on the Pacific Coast for about 4 months in what is now Oregon. Then they spent 6 months returning to St. Louis.

Write on Board

2. Have the students copy the following:

   Lewis and Clark Expedition (1804–1806)

   Went up the Missouri River from St. Louis

   Crossed mountains

   Reached the Pacific by sailing down the Columbia River

   Returned to St. Louis

3. Tell the class you want them to think for 2 minutes about what Lewis and Clark might have seen on their journey.

Write on Board

4. Compile on the board "Things That Lewis and Clark Might Have Seen." Have students copy the list or draw a picture about the Lewis and Clark expedition or do both.

Exercise 5: Standing Math: Addition

1. Divide the class in half, having each half face the other half in lines standing on opposite sides of the room.

2. Tell the class that they are going to do some addition problems.

Write on Board

3. Write 5 + 3 on the board.

4. Have 5 students step out from the front of the line on 1 side of the room, then have 3 students from the other side join them in the middle of the room.

5. Have the class count the students who have stepped out. Then complete the problem you have written on the board: $5 + 3 = 8$.

6. Have the 8 students return to their respective sides and go to the end of the line.

7. Repeat the process with each of the following problems, leaving the problems and their answers on the board. (Problems assume a class of 20 or more; eliminate problems that require an answer that is more than the number of students in the class.)

(1) $5 + 3 = 8$	(6) $7 + 2 = 9$	(11) $5 + 9 = 14$	(16) $1 + 2 = 3$
(2) $10 + 10 = 20$	(7) $4 + 7 = 11$	(12) $8 + 7 = 15$	(17) $8 + 6 = 14$
(3) $6 + 6 = 12$	(8) $8 + 5 = 13$	(13) $2 + 6 = 8$	(18) $10 + 7 = 17$
(4) $1 + 8 = 9$	(9) $9 + 7 = 16$	(14) $3 + 7 = 10$	(19) $7 + 7 = 14$
(5) $7 + 5 = 12$	(10) $4 + 1 = 5$	(15) $2 + 4 = 6$	(20) $3 + 9 = 12$

8. When the problems have been answered on the board, *erase the answers* but *not the problems.*

9. Have the students sit down, copy the problems, and answer them on their papers.

Exercise 6: Standing Math: Subtraction

1. Line up the entire class on 1 side of the room.

2. Tell the class that they are going to do some subtraction problems.

3. Write the number 5 on the board.

4. Have 5 students step out in front of the others from the head of the class line.

5. Write -3 after the 5.

6. Have 3 of the 5 students return to the back of the class line.

7. Have the class count the remaining 2 students, then complete the problem you have written on the board: $5 - 3 = 2$.

8. Have the remaining 2 students go to the back of the class line.

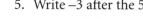

9. Repeat the process with each of the following problems, leaving the problems and their answers on the board. (This exercise assumes a class of 20 or more. Eliminate problems that require more students than the number of students in class.)

(1) $5 - 3 = 2$	(6) $7 - 3 = 4$	(11) $12 - 8 = 4$	(16) $17 - 6 = 11$
(2) $7 - 5 = 2$	(7) $16 - 4 = 12$	(12) $5 - 4 = 1$	(17) $19 - 12 = 7$
(3) $8 - 1 = 7$	(8) $11 - 9 = 2$	(13) $13 - 5 = 8$	(18) $9 - 5 = 4$
(4) $4 - 2 = 2$	(9) $6 - 3 = 3$	(14) $20 - 13 = 7$	(19) $6 - 5 = 1$
(5) $12 - 3 = 9$	(10) $9 - 9 = 0$	(15) $3 - 2 = 1$	(20) $10 - 2 = 8$

10. When the problems have all been answered on the board, *erase the answers* but *not the problems.*

11. Have the students sit down, copy the problems, and answer them on their papers.

Exercise 7: Standing Math: Multiplication

1. Line up the entire class on 1 side of the room.

2. Tell the class they are going to do some multiplication problems.

 3. Write 2×4 on the board.

4. Have 4 students step out from the head of the line as you say, "That is 1 times 4." Have another 4 students step out from the head of the line as you say, "That is 2 times 4."

5. Have the class count the students who have stepped out. Then complete the problem you have written on the board: $2 \times 4 = 8$.

6. Have the 8 students go to the end of the class line.

 7. Write 3×4 on the board.

8. Have 4 students step out from the head of the line as you say, "That is 1 times 4." Have another 4 students step out from the head of the line as you say, "That is 2 times 4." Have another 4 students step out from the head of the line as you say, "That is 3 times 4."

9. Have the class count the students who have stepped out. Then complete the problem you have written on the board: $3 \times 4 = 12$.

10. Have the 12 students go to the end of the class line.

 11. Repeat the process with each of the following problems, leaving the problems and their answers on the board. (This assumes a class of 20 or more; eliminate problems that require an answer that is more than the number of students in the class.)

(1) $2 \times 4 = 8$	(6) $1 \times 7 = 7$	(11) $2 \times 1 = 2$	(16) $6 \times 2 = 12$
(2) $3 \times 4 = 12$	(7) $7 \times 1 = 7$	(12) $8 \times 2 = 16$	(17) $3 \times 5 = 15$
(3) $4 \times 4 = 16$	(8) $4 \times 3 = 12$	(13) $3 \times 6 = 18$	(18) $2 \times 10 = 20$
(4) $2 \times 5 = 10$	(9) $4 \times 5 = 20$	(14) $7 \times 2 = 14$	(19) $2 \times 8 = 16$
(5) $2 \times 6 = 12$	(10) $2 \times 3 = 6$	(15) $2 \times 9 = 18$	(20) $10 \times 1 = 10$

12. When the problems have all been answered on the board, *erase the answers* but *not the problems.*

13. Have the students sit down, copy the problems, and answer them on their papers.

Exercise 8: Addition, Subtraction, Multiplication

1. Write the following problems on the board, without writing the answers. Have students copy all of the problems and then answer them on their papers.

(1) $10 + 3 = 13$	(8) $18 - 6 = 12$	(15) $2 \times 7 = 14$
(2) $11 + 4 = 15$	(9) $9 - 3 = 6$	(16) $3 \times 3 = 9$
(3) $7 + 12 = 19$	(10) $4 - 3 = 1$	(17) $3 \times 6 = 18$
(4) $6 + 7 = 13$	(11) $14 - 7 = 7$	(18) $5 \times 2 = 10$
(5) $14 + 3 = 17$	(12) $2 - 2 = 0$	(19) $9 \times 1 = 9$
(6) $2 + 9 = 11$	(13) $15 - 7 = 8$	(20) $6 \times 3 = 18$
(7) $10 + 10 = 20$	(14) $8 - 5 = 3$	(21) $2 \times 9 = 18$

2. When it appears that many in the class have completed the addition and the subtraction, have the entire class stand up. Permit the students to use their papers and answer as you ask each student for the answer to a problem. If the student misses, the student sits down and is asked no more questions. (It's like a spelldown, but you are using math problems instead of words.)

Exercise 9: James Madison

1. Read to the class:

James Madison is sometimes called the "Father of the Constitution" because he was responsible for much of what is in the Constitution. The Constitution is the basic set of rules for our government. The Constitution says we will have Congress, a president, and courts. It also contains a Bill of Rights that lists the basic rights of Americans. James Madison was a very good friend of Thomas Jefferson. After Thomas Jefferson was president for 8 years, James Madison was elected president. While he was president, we had our second war with England. This war was called the War of 1812, because that is the year it started. The British almost won the war when they captured Washington, D.C., and set fire to the President's House. President Madison and his wife, Dolley, were not in the house when it burned. They had already left Washington, D.C., to avoid being captured. While the British attacked Fort McHenry, in Baltimore, a lawyer named Francis Scott Key wrote "The Star-Spangled Banner." Key knew that the attack had failed when he saw our flag still waving. At the end of the war, General Andrew Jackson won a big victory for our side when the British tried to take New Orleans. By most accounts, James Madison was only about 5 feet 1 inch tall. He was a very serious person. His wife, Dolley, was taller and more fun-loving. She liked to hold parties and was very popular. One thing she liked to serve at her parties was ice cream.

2. Have students copy the following:

   James Madison (1751–1836)

   Wrote much of the U.S. Constitution

   Fourth president (1809–1817)

   President during the War of 1812

   "The Star-Spangled Banner" was written during the War of 1812.

3. Tell the class you want them to think for 2 minutes about what rights might be listed in the Bill of Rights.

4. Compile on the board a list of "Some Rights in the Bill of Rights" (religion, press, assembly, speech, jury trial, lawyer, and so on). Have the students copy the list or draw a picture about James Madison or do both.

Exercise 10: James Monroe

1. Read to the class:

James Monroe was the fifth president of the United States. When he was a teenager, he fought in the Revolutionary War under General George Washington. On Christmas night 1776, he and other American soldiers crossed the Delaware River in boats. They surprised the enemy soldiers and won a big victory against them the next morning. During the battle, James Monroe, who was 18 years old, was shot in the chest. His wound healed, and he continued to stay in the army. More than 40 years later, he became president. By then, men's clothes were different, but James Monroe continued to wear the same kinds of clothes that men had worn at the time of the Revolutionary War. He looked old-fashioned in his knee pants, long socks, and buckled shoes. Even though his clothing was out of date, he wanted the United States to be modern and powerful. While he was president, the United States got Florida from Spain. President Monroe told the world that North America and South America were places where European countries could no longer set up colonies. What he said became known as the Monroe Doctrine. James Monroe was president for 8 years. He lived for another 6 years and died on July 4, 1831. By then, 2 earlier presidents had also died on July 4: President John Adams and President Thomas Jefferson both died on July 4, 1826.

2. Have students copy the following:

   James Monroe (1758–1831)

   Wounded in the Revolutionary War

   Fifth president (1817–1825)

   U.S. got Florida (1819)

   Monroe Doctrine (1823)

3. Tell the class you want them to think for 2 minutes about Florida.

 4. Compile on the board a list of things about Florida. Have the students copy the list or draw a picture about James Monroe or do both.

Exercise 11: John Quincy Adams

 1. Read to the class:

John Quincy Adams was our sixth president. He was more successful before he became president and after he was president than he was while being president. Before becoming president he had done a good job representing America to foreign countries. His father, John Adams, had been the second president of the U.S., so it was expected that John Quincy Adams would make a good president. But when John Quincy became president, he wanted the U.S. to build so many things that he became very unpopular. Congress and many people at that time did not think the U.S. should spend money building a lot of roads, canals, and harbors. John Quincy's idea to build an observatory to study the stars was considered even crazier. John Quincy Adams was president for only 4 years. He tried to get elected for another 4 years, but he did not get enough votes. Two years later, he got enough votes to become a member of Congress. He was a member of Congress for 17 years and often spoke out against slavery. At the age of 80, he had a stroke and was carried from the floor of the House of Representatives into a small room off to the side, where he died.

 2. Have students copy the following:

John Quincy Adams (1767–1848)

Represented the U.S. to foreign countries

Sixth president (1825–1829)

Served in the U.S. House of Representatives (1831–1848)

Spoke out against slavery

3. Tell the class you want them to think for 2 minutes about why John Quincy Adams might have wanted roads, canals, harbors, and an observatory built back then.

4. Compile on the board a list of "Reasons to Build" roads, canals, harbors, and an observatory. Have the students copy the list or draw a picture about John Quincy Adams or do both.

Exercise 12: Erie Canal

Read Aloud 1. Read to the class:

Before there were trains, trucks, and airplanes to take goods from place to place, boats and horse-pulled or ox-pulled wagons transported things. When the Erie Canal opened for business in 1825, people thought it was wonderful because it meant that things could be sent by boat 360 miles between Buffalo, New York, and Albany, New York. The canal was only 4 feet deep, so the boats had flat bottoms and were often pulled by mules that walked along the bank beside the canal. Here are some of the words to a song that people sang about the canal.

Read Aloud 2. Read the following words to the class, along with the explanations:

(1) I've got a mule and her name is Sal

Fifteen miles on the Erie Canal

(2) She's a good old worker and a good old pal

Fifteen miles on the Erie Canal

(3) Get up there mule, here comes a lock

We'll make Rome about 6 o'clock

[Locks are places in canals where water is closed off by gates. They are used to raise boats by running water into the lock or to lower boats by draining water out of the lock. Rome, New York, was a town along the route of the canal.]

(4) One more trip and back we'll go

Right back home to Buffalo

(5) Low bridge, everybody down

Low bridge for we're goin' through a town

[People on the boat sometimes had to duck down when the boat went under a bridge.]

(6) And you'll always know your neighbor

You'll always know your pal

If you ever navigated on the Erie Canal

3. Have students listen to the selection as you read it again without the words of explanation.

4. Divide the class into 6 groups according to where they are sitting, numbering each group.

5. Say part 1; then have the entire class say part 1 in unison.

6. Have group 1 say part 1 in unison.

7. Tell group 1 that they are to remember part 1.

8. Repeat the process with the other parts: Say the part; then have the entire class say the part; then have the group say it.

9. Have each group repeat its part from memory, putting the entire selection together; then have the entire class say the entire selection in unison from memory.

Exercise 13: Sunshine, Temperature

Read Aloud

1. Read to the class:

Weather on Earth begins with the Sun. Although the Sun is about 93 million miles away from Earth, it is so big and so hot that it gives us the light and heat we have on Earth. The Sun's size (mass) is 330,000 times larger than Earth. Its temperature on the surface is usually more than 9,900 degrees Fahrenheit. By comparison, the Earth's average is about 59 degrees Fahrenheit. It takes the rays of the Sun about 8 minutes to reach the Earth. The rays travel at 186,000 miles per second. If an automobile could travel that fast it would go around the Earth about $7\frac{1}{2}$ times in a second. Sunshine heats up the Earth; thus, it is hotter during the day for the half of the Earth that is facing the Sun and colder at night for the half of the Earth that is not facing the Sun. Earth temperatures change according to how close the Earth is to the Sun.

It takes 365 days for the Earth to go completely around the Sun. During that time we have our seasons. As the Earth moves around the Sun, the Earth is spinning like a top. The Earth tips at various angles to the Sun, just as you might tip a full carton of milk to pour milk into a glass. Places on Earth tipped toward the Sun are in summer; places tipped away from the Sun are in winter.

A very hot temperature of 136 degrees Fahrenheit was recorded in Libya in 1922. A very cold temperature of −129 degrees Fahrenheit was recorded in Antarctica in 1983.

Write on Board

2. Have the students copy the following:

The weather on Earth begins with the Sun.

The Sun is much bigger and hotter than the Earth.

Sun rays bring light and heat to the Earth.

Sun rays travel at 186,000 miles per second.

Seasons change as a place tips toward or away from the Sun.

3. Tell the class you want them to think for 2 minutes about how sunshine affects each of them.

Write on Board

4. Compile on the board a list of "How Sunshine Affects Us." Have students copy the list or draw a picture about sunshine or do both.

Exercise 14: Winds, Fronts

Read Aloud

1. Read to the class:

The rays of the Sun reach the Earth at different places at different angles. When the Sun heats up a particular place, the hot air rises, creating an area of *low pressure.* Cold air falls, creating a *high pressure* area. Cold air shifts into areas where hot air is rising. The heating, cooling, and shifting air creates winds. When a large mass of cold air is moving someplace, it is called a *cold front.* When a large mass of warm air is blowing someplace, it is called a *warm front.* Sometimes cold fronts and warm fronts abruptly bump into each other. When they do, we have high winds and sometimes violent weather. The TV weather people sometimes talk about the *jet stream.* These are winds about 6 miles above the Earth that usually travel at about 125 miles per hour, but they can go twice that fast. One jet stream circles the top half of the Earth, the other the bottom half. When jet streams change course they cause weather changes on the Earth's surface. In the state of New Hampshire in 1934 a surface wind speed of 231 miles per hour was recorded, perhaps the strongest Earth wind on record.

Write on Board

2. Have students copy the following:

Hot air rises and creates low pressure.

Cold air falls and creates high pressure.

Cold fronts and warm fronts can shift from place to place.

The heating, cooling, and shifting air creates winds.

3. Tell the class you want them to think for 2 minutes about how wind affects them.

Write on Board

4. Compile on the board a list of "How Wind Affects Us." Have students copy the list or draw a picture about wind or do both.

Exercise 15: Clouds, Fog

Read Aloud

1. Read to the class:

Over two-thirds of the Earth's surface is covered by water. Although you can't see it, water is even in the air around us. The water in the air is called *humidity. High humidity* means that there is a lot of water in the air; *low humidity* means there is little water in the air. When air heats up, it rises. Cold air pushing under warm air will also force warm air up. Sometimes warm air rises when wind pushes up to go over mountains. As warm air rises, it gets cooler. As it keeps getting higher and cooler, the water vapor changes form, condensing to mist and droplets of water by attaching itself to small bits of dust or smoke or any small particles that are floating in the sky. When the cloud gets heavy enough with water, it drops the water back down to the surface of the Earth in the form of rain, snow, sleet, or hail. The air picks up the water vapor and carries it back into the sky. This action makes more clouds form. We have a continuous cycle of air taking water up and dropping it back down. Fog is a cloud that has formed near the ground. The cloud is formed when air that is full of a lot of water vapor comes into contact with the ground or with surface water that has a very different temperature. When the temperature warms up enough, the fog disappears because it turns back into invisible water vapor.

 2. Have students copy the following:

As warm air rises it gets cooler.

As warm air rises and gets cooler, water vapor condenses into mist and water droplets.

The mist and water droplets form clouds.

The clouds drop the water back down.

Clouds that form near the ground are called fog.

3. Tell the class that you want them to think for 2 minutes about how clouds affect them.

 4. Compile on the board a list of "How Clouds Affect Us." Have students copy the list or draw a picture about clouds or do both.

Exercise 16: Dew, Frost, Ice

 1. Read to the class:

Have you ever walked in the grass in the early morning in your bare feet? Your feet become wet. The moisture on the grass is what we call *dew*. If the weather is cold enough, the dew freezes and we call it *frost*. When the Sun goes down, the ground loses heat faster than the air. As the invisible water vapor that is in the air near the ground cools down, it changes form. It condenses into droplets of water. If the temperature drops to 32 degrees Fahrenheit or less, it becomes frost. Sometimes frost is even on the trees. If you leave your dog's or cat's bowl of water outside at night and the temperature drops to 32 degrees Fahrenheit or lower, the water will turn to ice on the top of the bowl. The colder it gets the deeper down into the bowl it will freeze. The water under the layer of ice does not freeze because it is warmer than the ice on top. If it gets really cold, all of the water in the bowl will turn to ice. Dew, frost, and ice are all water. The only difference is temperature.

2. Have the students copy the following:

The ground at night loses heat faster than air loses heat.

Invisible water vapor in the air condenses into droplets of water.

Above 32 degrees Fahrenheit, the droplets are dew.

At 32 degrees Fahrenheit or below, the water droplets are frost.

Ice is frozen water.

3. Tell the class you want them to think for 2 minutes about how dew, frost, and ice affect them.

4. Compile on the board a list of "How Dew, Frost, and Ice Affect Us." Have students copy the list or draw a picture about dew, frost, or ice, or do both.

Exercise 17: Andrew Jackson

1. Read to the class:

When the British invaded South Carolina, Andrew Jackson's family was caught up in the Revolutionary War. At the age of 13 Andrew joined the American army and was captured by the British. Andrew's father had died the year he was born, and his mother did not survive the Revolutionary War. Andrew became an orphan at the age of 14. By the age of 20 he had become a lawyer. He was elected and appointed to many important jobs. He also was a soldier for much of his life. When he was a general in the War of 1812, the men under his command won a big victory when the British tried to take New Orleans. Defeating the British at the battle of New Orleans made Jackson so well-known and popular that he was eventually elected president.

Ordinary people liked Jackson because he had started out as an orphan and had made it all the way to the presidency. Andrew Jackson was a forceful president. He made the state of South Carolina obey the laws made in Washington, D.C., even though South Carolina said it would obey only the laws it wanted to obey. President Jackson also forced American Indians in the East to move west of the Mississippi River. Later, the Indian Territory they moved to became the state of Oklahoma.

Andrew Jackson was in poor health in his older years. Sometimes he coughed up blood. That's because there was a bullet in him. Years before, he had been in a duel with another man. In the duel Jackson and the other man had stood with their backs to each other. Then they had walked a number of steps away from each other and turned to fire their pistols. The other man fired first and his bullet struck Jackson in the chest. Even though he was shot, Jackson took careful aim at the other man and killed him.

2. Have students copy the following:

Andrew Jackson (1767–1845)

Defeated the British at the Battle of New Orleans

Seventh president (1829–1837)

Forced South Carolina to obey laws made in Washington, D.C.

Had American Indians moved west of the Mississippi River

3. Tell the class you want them to think for 2 minutes about how they think Andrew Jackson went from orphan to president.

 4. Compile on the board a list of "How Andrew Jackson Became President" (hard work, studied, became hero, and so on). Have students copy the list or draw a picture about Andrew Jackson or do both.

Exercise 18: Martin Van Buren

 1. Read to the class:

Martin Van Buren was the first president who had been born a citizen of the United States. All of the presidents before him had been born before the United States had become a country. Van Buren was also the first president of Dutch ancestry. Van Buren was very interested in politics and was good at getting people elected. He could convince people to support the candidate he supported. He helped Andrew Jackson get elected president. Four years later, he helped Jackson get elected again. This time, he became Jackson's vice president. When Jackson was finishing his eight years as president, he told people that they should elect Martin Van Buren as president. Van Buren was elected president. When he moved into the White House, his four grown sons, ages 20, 25, 27, and 30, also moved in. Van Buren's wife had died many years earlier, and he had not remarried. Van Buren wasn't as popular as Jackson had been. When Van Buren became president, the country went through a *depression,* which means that a whole bunch of people lost their jobs. Van Buren could not get elected a second term.

 2. Have students copy the following:

Martin Van Buren (1791–1868)

Knew how to get people elected

Eighth president (1837–1841)

People lost jobs (there was a depression).

Did not get reelected

3. Tell the class that you want them to think for 2 minutes about whether or not grown children should live with their parents.

 4. Compile on the board a list of "Yes" and "No" reasons for whether grown children should live with their parents. Have students copy the list or draw a picture about Martin Van Buren or do both.

Exercise 19: William Henry Harrison

1. Read to the class:

William Henry Harrison had been a soldier much of his life. When he tried to become president, his campaign used the slogan "Tippecanoe and Tyler too." Tippecanoe was a river where troops commanded by Harrison had won a battle against Shawnee American Indians. The leader of the Shawnees, Tecumseh, wanted all American Indian tribes to unite and drive whites out of the places they were settling. The "Tyler" in the slogan referred to John Tyler, who was running as vice president.

When 68-year-old William Henry Harrison was sworn in, he gave a long speech outside on a cold, windy, rainy day. He caught pneumonia and died 1 month after he became president. Because he was the first president to die while being president, there was a lot of figuring out what to do. One of the things that had to be decided was where and how to hold the funeral. The White House was draped in black curtains. The president's body was put on display in a coffin with a glass window so that people could pass by and pay their respects. The funeral was held in the White House. The coffin was taken out of the White House and put on a funeral wagon pulled by horses that had black cloth draped over them. The Marine Band played sad songs and soldiers fired cannons. The wagon was pulled to a cemetery and stayed there a short time while waiting for a train to arrive. Then the funeral train took Harrison's body to his home state of Ohio for burial. This set the pattern that most funerals would follow when a president dies while being president.

2. Have students copy the following:

   William Henry Harrison (1773–1841)

   Campaign slogan "Tippecanoe and Tyler too"

   Ninth president (March 4, 1841 to April 4, 1841)

   Died 1 month after becoming president

3. Tell the class you want them to think for 2 minutes about what each of them would use for a campaign slogan if they tried to become president. (Example: "Don't miss, vote for Chris.")

4. Compile on the board a list of their campaign slogans. Have students copy the list or draw a picture about William Henry Harrison or do both.

Exercise 20: Oklahoma

1. Read to the class:

American settlers and American Indians fought each other off and on for many years. President Andrew Jackson thought that a good way to solve the problem was to make the American Indians move to a place where there weren't any settlers; so he ordered the American Indian tribes who were living east of the Mississippi River to move west of the river. Many of the American Indians did not want to go. Some of the tribes felt it was just a way for settlers to get the land the Indians had been living on. The Indians were forced to go, and their trip was called "The Trail of Tears." Later, settlers were allowed to move into parts of the Indian Territory. In 1907, the territory became the state of Oklahoma. Oil was discovered in Oklahoma and some people got rich. Oklahoma remains the headquarters for a large number of American Indian tribes. Its state name, like the names of many other states, rivers, cities, and other things, is of American Indian origin. *Oklahoma* means *red man* in the Choctaw Indian language.

2. Have students copy the following:

Oklahoma

Native Americans moved there from east of the Mississippi.

Territory was opened to settlement of non-Indians.

Became the forty-sixth state in 1907

Discovery of oil made some people rich

Oklahoma means "red man" in Choctaw.

3. Have each student draw a picture about Oklahoma and have students show their pictures to the class.

Exercise 21: Rain, Snow, Sleet, Hail

1. Read to the class:

Rain, snow, sleet, and hail all come from clouds. What makes the difference in what they are is temperature in the cloud as well as temperature between the cloud and the ground. Much of the time rain starts out as snow and it turns to rain as it falls through the air. If the air is cold enough, it remains snow. Sleet is half-frozen rain or half-melted snow. Hail is moisture, as are rain, snow, and sleet, but it is formed differently. It is made inside clouds that are much warmer at the bottom than at the top. The difference in temperature causes the raindrops to rise from the warm bottom and freeze at the cold top. This creates a popcorn-popper effect, bouncing the raindrops up and down, building freezing layers of ice on them until they get heavy enough to fall as hail. A hailstone fell in Aurora, Nebraska, on June 22, 2003. It was 18 inches around and 7 inches across. The island of Kauai in Hawaii has a mountain that may be the wettest place on Earth. It rains about 350 days a year and gets an average of 460 inches of rain each year.

2. Have students copy the following:

Temperature determines whether condensed water vapor will be rain, snow, or sleet.

Hail is formed inside a cloud that is warm at the bottom and cold at the top.

Raindrops pop up and down inside a cloud to form hail.

Each time the raindrop pops up into the colder part of the cloud, it becomes heavier with more ice.

When a raindrop gets heavy enough with ice it falls to the ground as a hailstone.

3. Tell the students you want them to think for 2 minutes about how rain, snow, sleet, and hail affect them.

 4. Compile on the board a list of "How Rain, Snow, Sleet, and Hail Affect Us." Have students copy the list or draw a picture about rain, snow, sleet, or hail, or do both.

Exercise 22: Lightning, Thunder

 1. Read to the class:

Have you ever accidentally *shocked* somebody by scraping your feet on the carpet and then touching them with your finger? An electrical charge went from you to them. Electrons from your body wanted to join electrons that were not part of your body. That is somewhat how lightning works. Sometimes electrons will join other electrons by flashing across the inside of a cloud. Sometimes they will join other electrons by flashing from cloud to cloud. Sometimes they will flash to the ground to join other electrons. Hail inside a cloud creates lightning. Hail forms inside clouds when the bottom of the cloud is much warmer than the top of the cloud. The difference in temperature causes raindrops to bounce up and down, turning the raindrops into hail as a layer of ice is added each time they bounce up. As the raindrops that are changing to hail pop up and down, they bump together. This causes electrical charges to build up inside the cloud. Electrical charges, electrons, want to join other electrical charges. A lightning flash is electrons on their way to join other electrons. When lightning flashes, it heats up the air around it so fast and so much that as the air splits apart it makes a loud noise. We call that loud noise *thunder.* You see the lightning before you hear the clap of thunder because light travels faster than sound.

 2. Have students copy the following:

As forming hail bumps together inside a cloud, electrical charges build up.

Flashes of lightning are electrons speeding to join other electrons.

Thunder is caused by speeding electrons heating and splitting the air.

Light travels faster than sound.

3. Tell the students you want them to think for 2 minutes about how lightning and thunder affect them.

 4. Compile on the board a list of "How Lightning and Thunder Affect Us." Have students copy the list or draw a picture about lightning and thunder or do both.

Exercise 23: Tornadoes, Hurricanes

 1. Read to the class:

Tornadoes and hurricanes are both swirling wind. Both develop when temperatures are very warm. Tornadoes start as columns of warm air quickly stretching up from the ground. Strong winds can start the column of wind spinning. Hurricanes start when a part of the ocean and the air above it are heated up. The rising warm air creates a low pressure area that surrounding air is sucked into, and this causes fierce winds. A tornado may be a few feet across to several hundred feet across. Hurricanes are much larger. They may be as big as 300 miles across. The center of a hurricane is called the *eye*. The air pressure there is very low and causes the wind to swirl around. The wind in tornadoes usually spins much faster than the wind in hurricanes. Both tornadoes and hurricanes can travel great distances, sucking up things in their path as they move along. Eventually, with temperature changes and changes in location, the winds die down and the tornado or hurricane ends, often leaving behind a lot of destruction. On rare occasions, a tornado forms over a body of water. Then it is called a *waterspout,* because water is sucked up inside the spinning wind and it looks like a very tall fountain shooting up into the sky. Tornadoes are not given names. This is probably because there are so many of them and they are sometimes very small. Hurricanes used to not be named. Then people started giving them girls' names. Now they give hurricanes either a boy's name or a girl's name.

 2. Have the students copy the following:

Tornadoes and hurricanes are swirling wind.

They form when temperatures are very warm.

Tornadoes are smaller than hurricanes and usually form over land.

Hurricanes usually have lower wind speeds than tornadoes but are larger.

Both can be very destructive.

3. Tell the students you want them to think for 2 minutes about how tornadoes and hurricanes affect the way people live.

 4. Compile on the board a list of "How Tornadoes and Hurricanes Affect People." Have students copy the list or draw a picture about tornadoes or hurricanes or do both.

Exercise 24: TV Weather Person

1. Tell the class that you want them to pretend that each of them is a TV weather person. Have them take out a piece of paper, and down the left-hand side of the paper have them write M, T, W, T, F, leaving 3 lines between each letter. Tell them that each of them is to make up a 5-day weather forecast, giving daytime highs and nighttime lows, as well as other important information about what the weather will be like. They are to jot down anything on each day of the week that will help them to remember their forecast. They might even want to make little drawings beside each day of the week, showing clouds or whatever, to show the weather.

2. After about 15 minutes or so, depending on how many are ready, have individual students stand up and give a weather forecast.

Chapter Five

Third Grade Lesson Plans

Exercise 1: States 1–13

1. As you read state names and explanations, have students copy the name of each state and the date it was admitted to the Union. (The date of admission for the original 13 was the date each state ratified the U.S. Constitution.)

(1) Delaware (Dec. 7, 1787). Named for Lord De La Ware, early governor of Virginia. Later the name was applied to a river and an American Indian tribe.

(2) Pennsylvania (Dec. 12, 1787). Named for William Penn, founder of Pennsylvania (means Penn's forest).

(3) New Jersey (Dec. 18, 1787). Named after England's Isle of Jersey.

(4) Georgia (Jan. 2, 1788). Named for King George of England.

(5) Connecticut (Jan. 9, 1788). American Indian, "long river place" in Mohican and Algonquin.

(6) Massachusetts (Feb. 6, 1788). American Indian, "large hill place."

(7) Maryland (Apr. 28, 1788). Named for Queen Henrietta Maria, wife of King Charles I of England.

(8) South Carolina (May 23, 1788). Named for King Charles I of England. *Corolus* is Latin for "Charles."

(9) New Hampshire (June 21, 1788). Named after a county in England.

(10) Virginia (June 25, 1788). Named for Queen Elizabeth I of England, who was called the "Virgin Queen" because she never married.

(11) New York (June 26, 1788). Named after the Duke of York of England.

(12) North Carolina (Nov. 21, 1789). Named for King Charles I of England. *Corolus* is Latin for "Charles."

(13) Rhode Island (May 29, 1790). Exact origin unknown, but it may have been "red island" in Dutch because of red clay soil.

 Read Aloud 2. Have students turn over their papers and use a new sheet of paper to take a spelling test as you read state names.

3. Have students check their papers by comparing them with the paper on which they had written the state names previously.

Read Aloud 4. Have students turn over both papers and write on the back of the paper on which they just took the spelling test. Read explanations of the states (but not the names of the states), and have students write the name of the state as you read the explanation.

5. Have students check their papers.

Exercise 2: States 14–26

Write on Board

Read Aloud 1. As you read state names and explanations, have students copy the name of each state and the date it was admitted to the Union:

(14) Vermont (Mar. 4, 1791). From French words *vert* (green) and *mont* (mountain).

(15) Kentucky (June 1, 1792). American Indian, various translations, "dark and bloody ground," "land of tomorrow," "meadowland."

(16) Tennessee (June 1, 1796). American Indian, named after Cherokee villages called "Tanasi."

(17) Ohio (Mar. 1, 1803). American Indian, Iroquois for "fine (or good) river."

(18) Louisiana (Apr. 30, 1812). Named for King Louis XIV of France.

(19) Indiana (Dec. 11, 1816). Means land of the Indians.

(20) Mississippi (Dec. 10, 1817). American Indian, Chippewa for "great river" or "gathering of all waters," Algonquin word "messipi."

(21) Illinois (Dec. 3, 1818). Named for the Illinois River, which was named by French explorers for Indians living on the banks of the river.

(22) Alabama (Dec. 14, 1819). American Indian, tribal town, "Alabamas" tribe.

(23) Maine (May 15, 1820). Named after an ancient French province. Means "mainland."

(24) Missouri (Aug. 10, 1821). American Indian, Algonquin for "river of big canoes."

(25) Arkansas (June 15, 1836). American Indian, "south wind," from Algonquin name for Quapaw Indians.

(26) Michigan (June 26, 1837). American Indian, Chippewa words "mici gama" meaning "great water."

2. Have students turn over their papers and use a new sheet of paper to take a spelling test as you read state names.

3. Have students check their papers by comparing them with the paper on which they wrote the state names.

4. Have students turn over both papers and write on the back of the paper on which they just took the spelling test. Read the explanations of the states (but not the names of the states), and have students write the name of the state as you read the explanation.

5. Have students check their papers.

Exercise 3: States 27–38

1. As you read state names and explanations, have students copy the name of each state and the date it was admitted to the Union:

(27) Florida (Mar. 3, 1845). Spanish, "Pescua Florida" for "Flowery Easter."

(28) Texas (Dec. 29, 1845). American Indian, meaning "friends" or "allies." Then Caddo Indians were called that by the Spanish. Also written "Texias," "Tejas," "Teysas."

(29) Iowa (Dec. 28, 1846). American Indian, from Iowa Indian word meaning "here I rest" or "beautiful land."

(30) Wisconsin (May 29, 1848). American Indian, from Chippewa word meaning "grassy place."

(31) California (Sept. 9, 1850). Spanish name for an imaginary island that was paradise on earth.

(32) Minnesota (Mar. 11, 1858). American Indian, Dakota Sioux word meaning "cloudy water" or "sky-tinted water."

(33) Oregon (Feb. 14, 1859). Origin of name is uncertain. Possibly named after the river that Indians called *Ouragen.*

(34) Kansas (Jan. 29, 1861). American Indian, Sioux word for "south wind people."

(35) West Virginia (June 20, 1863). Called "West Virginia" when it separated from Virginia in the Civil War.

(36) Nevada (Oct. 31, 1864). Spanish, meaning "snow-clad."

(37) Nebraska (Mar. 1, 1867). American Indian, Omaha or Otos Indian word meaning "broad water" or "flat river."

(38) Colorado (Aug. 1, 1876). From Spanish for "color red."

2. Have students turn over their papers and use a new sheet of paper to take a spelling test as you read state names.

3. Have students check their papers by comparing them with the paper on which they wrote the state names.

4. Have students turn over both papers and write on the back of the paper on which they just took the spelling test. Read explanations of the states (but not the names of the states), and have students write the name of the state as you read the explanation.

5. Have students check their papers.

Exercise 4: States 39–50

1. As you read state names and explanations, have students copy the name of each state and the date it was admitted to the Union:

(39) North Dakota (Nov. 2, 1889). American Indian; "Dakota" is Sioux for "friend" or "ally."

(40) South Dakota (Nov. 2, 1889). American Indian; "Dakota" is Sioux for "friend" or "ally."

(41) Montana (Nov. 8, 1889). Latin or Spanish for "mountainous."

(42) Washington (Nov. 11, 1889). Named for George Washington.

(43) Idaho (July 3, 1890). Possibly an invented word that means "gem of the mountains" or a Kiowa Apache Indian term for the Comanche Indians.

(44) Wyoming (July 10, 1890). American Indian; Algonquin for "large prairie" or "big plains."

(45) Utah (Jan. 4, 1896). American Indian, from a Navajo word meaning "upper" or "higher up." A Shoshone tribe was called "Ute."

(46) Oklahoma (Nov. 16, 1907). American Indian; means "red man" in Choctaw.

(47) New Mexico (Jan. 6, 1912). The Spanish in Mexico in the 1500s started calling the area farther north by this name.

(48) Arizona (Feb. 14, 1912). Possibly the Spanish version of the Aztec Indian word "arizuma," meaning "silver bearing." Another possibility is that it came from the Spanish version of a Pima Indian word for "little spring place."

(49) Alaska (Jan. 3, 1959). Russian version of Aleutian (Eskimo) word for "peninsula," "great lands," or "land that is not an island."

(50) Hawaii (Aug. 21, 1959). Possibly comes from Native Hawaiian word of "Hawaiki" or "Owhyhee," meaning "homeland."

2. Have students turn over their papers and use a new sheet of paper to take a spelling test as you read the state names.

3. Have students check their papers by comparing them with the paper on which they wrote the state names.

4. Have students turn over both papers and write on the back of the paper on which they just took the spelling test. Read explanations of the states (but not the names of the states), and have students write the name of the state as you read the explanation.

5. Have students check their papers.

Exercise 5: John Tyler

 1. Read to the class:

The president and vice president of the United States have a term of office of 4 years. During that 4-year period, we say that the president and vice president are "in office." When President William Henry Harrison died a month after becoming president, Vice President John Tyler became president. Because it was the first time a president had died in office, people weren't sure how long John Tyler should be president. Was he just acting as president until an election could be held, or was he president until the end of Harrison's term of office? John Tyler answered that question firmly by saying that he was not just a temporary president. He served out the rest of what would have been William Henry Harrison's time in office.

John Tyler's wife died while he was president, and he married a woman 30 years younger than he was. He was the father of 8 children with his first wife and then another 7 with his second wife. While he was president a serious accident took place on a ship that was carrying him and a lot of important visitors. When one of the ship's guns was fired, the gun blew up, killing a number of people and injuring others. The president escaped injury but the Secretary of State and the Secretary of the Navy were among those who died. Also killed was the father of Julia Gardiner, the young woman who became John Tyler's second wife. Julia was on the ship but she had no injuries. It was President Tyler's consoling her for the loss of her father that probably led to their marriage.

John Tyler didn't get along with most of the members of the government, but he did manage to get Congress to cooperate with him on 2 very important measures. One settled the boundary between the state of Maine and Canada, which was then under control of the British. The other was a resolution that Texas would be admitted as a state, which it was shortly after John Tyler left office.

 2. Have students copy the following:

John Tyler (1790–1862)

Became president when President William Henry Harrison died

Tenth president (1841–1845)

Fathered more children than any other president

Helped get Congress to approve Texas becoming a state

Helped settle the boundary between state of Maine and Canada

3. Have each student compose 3 sentences about John Tyler and sketch a picture illustrating the sentences.

4. Have students read their sentences to the class and show their drawings.

Exercise 6: James Knox Polk

Read Aloud))) 1. Read to the class:

James Knox Polk came into office at the time when Texas was being admitted to the U.S. as a state. Texas had won its independence from Mexico 9 years earlier, and Mexico was still unhappy about losing Texas. President Polk was eager to add new territory to the U.S. The U.S. and Mexico disagreed about where the border between the two countries should be. The U.S. said the border was the Rio Grande River. Mexico said it was the Nueces River. Both countries sent soldiers into the disputed area and the 2 countries started fighting. The fighting ended when the U.S. captured Mexico City and won the war. The U.S. got from Mexico the land that is now the southwest part of the U.S. President Polk's term of office also included working out a treaty with Great Britain that established the boundary between the U.S. and Canada where the present-day state of Washington is.

James Polk and his wife, Sarah, had no children. Sarah Polk banned dancing and serving alcoholic beverages at the White House. She believed they were inappropriate for the White House. President Polk worked very hard and exhausted himself during his 4 years in office. He returned home to Tennessee, hoping to have a restful retirement. He died at the age of 53, only 3 months after leaving office.

 2. Have students copy the following:

James Knox Polk (1795–1849)

Eleventh president (1845–1849)

President during the Mexican War (1846–1848)

U.S. acquired what is now the Southwest part of the U.S.

Settled boundary between Canada and where the present-day state of Washington is

Very hard-working president

3. Have each student compose 3 sentences about James Knox Polk and sketch a picture illustrating the sentences.

4. Have students read their sentences to the class and show their drawings.

Exercise 7: Zachary Taylor

1. Read to the class:

Zachary Taylor was so uninterested in politics that he had never even voted until people started wanting him to run for president. Zachary Taylor was a career soldier who had fought in the War of 1812 and then fought many battles with American Indians. He earned great fame and popularity in the Mexican War. Mexican General Antonio Lopez de Santa Anna had nearly 4 times as many soldiers as General Taylor at Buena Vista. Santa Anna asked Taylor to surrender. Taylor refused and won the battle. Taylor was the kind of soldier who didn't care much for dressing up in fine uniforms, and he often looked disheveled and sloppy. The soldiers under Taylor's command were very fond of him and referred to him as "Old Rough and Ready."

After the Mexican War Taylor was asked to run for president and he did. When President Taylor moved to the White House, he took "Whitey," his favorite horse, with him. Whitey was allowed to roam the White House grounds, feeding on the grass.

President Taylor surprised many southern slave owners by not trying to extend slavery into the new territories. With all of the new territory that had been gained in winning the war against Mexico, southerners thought that California and other places new to the United States should be allowed to become states where people could own slaves. Taylor was a southerner and he owned slaves, but he was willing to let territories become states even if they didn't permit people to own slaves.

Sixteen months after taking office President Taylor attended a Fourth of July celebration. He ate a lot of fruit and vegetables, drank a lot of milk, and got very hot. He got very sick, possibly from what he ate and drank and maybe from the heat. He died 5 days later.

2. Have students copy the following:

   Zachary Taylor (1784–1850)

   Nickname "Old Rough and Ready" and became a hero in the Mexican War

   Twelfth president (1849–1850)

   Wanted to admit new states even if the new states banned slavery

   Died 16 months after taking office

3. Have each student compose 3 sentences about Zachary Taylor and sketch a picture illustrating the sentences.

4. Have students read their sentences to the class and show their drawings.

Exercise 8: Texas

Read Aloud))

1. Read to the class:

In the early days American Indians lived in Texas. Then the Spanish claimed it, but they had trouble taking control from the Indian tribes. Mexico revolted against Spain and became a separate country, with Texas becoming a part of Mexico. Settlers from the U.S. began moving into Texas, and not many years passed before the American settlers and Mexican authorities started feuding. The Texans revolted against Mexico, and in 1836 with cries of "Remember the Alamo!" won independence from Mexico. The Alamo was where nearly 200 Texans had died in a battle against Mexican soldiers.

For 9 years Texas was a country called the "Republic of Texas" and sometimes the "Lone Star Republic." Then in 1845 Texas was admitted into the United States as the twenty-eighth state. Austin, the capital of Texas, is named after Stephen Austin, who was the leader of the first group of American settlers in Texas. Houston is named after Sam Houston, who defeated General Antonio Lopez de Santa Anna at the battle of San Jacinto. That was the battle that won Texas its independence from Mexico. Texas was the largest state in the United States for over 100 years, until Alaska became a state in 1959.

Write on Board

2. Have students copy the following:

Texas

Won independence from Mexico in 1836

Was the country called "Republic of Texas" for 9 years

Admitted to the U.S. as the twenty-eighth state in 1845

Austin, the capital, named for Stephen Austin

Houston named for Sam Houston

3. Have each student compose 3 sentences about Texas and sketch a picture illustrating the sentences.

4. Have students read their sentences and show their drawings to the class.

Exercise 9: Money Math: Addition

Write on Board

1. Write on the board and have students copy the following, informing them that these are the faces on our paper money:

$1 George Washington (GW)

$2 Thomas Jefferson (TJ)

$5 Abraham Lincoln (AL)

$10 Alexander Hamilton (AH)

$20 Andrew Jackson (AJ)

$50 Ulysses Grant (UG)

$100 Ben Franklin (BF)

2. Write on the board and have students copy the following 10 *addition* problems and work them:

1.	one TJ	$ 2	2.	three GW		3.	two BF	
	+ two AJ	$40		+ two AL	___		+ one AJ	___
		$42						

4.	one AH		5.	four AL		6.	seven GW	
	+ one UG	___		+ two UG	___		+ three TJ	___

7.	two AJ		8.	six AH		9.	five GW	
	+ two AJ	___		+ one UG	___		+ two AL	___

10.   five BF

       + seven TJ   ___

3. Have students check their papers as you read the answers:

1. ($42)	2. ($13)	3. ($220)
4. ($60)	5. ($120)	6. ($13)
7. ($80)	8. ($110)	9. ($15)
10. ($514)		

4. Have each student compose 5 math money addition problems and answer them.

Exercise 10: Money Math: Subtraction

1. Write on the board and have students copy the following, informing them that these pictures are on the back of our paper money:

$1 Great Seal of the U.S. (GS)

$2 Signers of Declaration of Independence (SD)

$5 Lincoln Memorial (LM)

$10 U.S. Treasury (UST)

$20 White House (WH)

$50 U.S. Capitol (USC)

$100 Independence Hall (IH)

2. Write on the board and have students copy the following *subtraction* problems and work them:

<table>
<tr><td>1.   three GS $3
   – <u>one SD</u> $2
           $1</td><td>2.   one IH
   – <u>two WH</u> ___</td><td>3.   three WH
   – <u>five LM</u> ___</td></tr>
<tr><td>4.   twenty GS
   – <u>one UST</u> ___</td><td>5.   five IH
   – <u>ten UST</u> ___</td><td>6.   three USC
   – <u>seven SD</u> ___</td></tr>
<tr><td>7.   seven UST
   – <u>six SD</u> ___</td><td>8.   four SD
   – <u>six GS</u> ___</td><td>9.   four WH
   – <u>three UST</u> ___</td></tr>
<tr><td>10.   six USC
   – <u>two IH</u> ___</td><td></td><td></td></tr>
</table>

Read Aloud 3. Have students check their papers as you read the answers:

1. ($1)	2. ($60)	3. ($35)
4. ($10)	5. ($400)	6. ($136)
7. ($58)	8. ($2)	9. ($50)
10. ($100)		

4. Have each student compose 5 money math subtraction problems and answer them.

Exercise 11: Money Math: Multiplication

Write on Board 1. Write on the board and have the students copy the following, informing them that these are the faces and the pictures on our paper money:

$1 George Washington, Great Seal (GWGS)

$2 Thomas Jefferson, Signers of the Declaration of Independence (TJSD)

$5 Abraham Lincoln, Lincoln Memorial (ALLM)

$10 Alexander Hamilton, U.S. Treasury (AHUST)

$20 Andrew Jackson, White House (AJWH)

$50 Ulysses Grant, U.S. Capitol (UGUSC)

$100 Benjamin Franklin, Independence Hall (BFIH)

2. Write on the board and have students copy the following *multiplication* problems and work them:

1. three GWGS	$3	2. one UGUSC	3. one BFIH	
× two TJSD	$4	× two TJSD ___	× two TJSD ___	
	$12			

4. one AJWH   5. five ALLM   6. two UGUSC
   × two GWGS ___   × five GWGS ___   × two TJSD ___

7. three AHUST   8. two BFIH   9. six GWGS
   × one ALLM ___   × one ALLM ___   × four TJSD ___

10. five AJWH
    × one BFIH ___

3. Have students check their papers as you read the answers:

1. ($12)   2. ($200)   3. ($400)
4. ($40)   5. ($125)   6. ($400)
7. ($150)   8. ($1000)   9. ($48)
10. ($10,000)

4. Have each student compose 5 money math multiplication problems and answer them.

Exercise 12: Money Math: Addition, Subtraction, Multiplication

1. Write on the board and have students copy the following, informing them that these are the faces and the pictures on our paper money:

$1 George Washington, Great Seal (GWGS)

$2 Thomas Jefferson, Signers of the Declaration of Independence (TJSD)

$5 Abraham Lincoln, Lincoln Memorial (ALLM)

$10 Alexander Hamilton, U.S. Treasury (AHUST)

$20 Andrew Jackson, White House (AJWH)

$50 Ulysses Grant, U.S. Capitol (UGUSC)

$100 Benjamin Franklin, Independence Hall (BFIH)

2. Write on the board and have students copy the following problems and work them:

1.	six GWGS	$ 6	2.	five TJSD	$ 10	3.	five BFIH	$ 500
	× four TJSD	$ 8		+ one TJSD	$ 2		– two AHUST	$ 20
		$ 48			$ 12			$ 480

4.	six AHUST		5.	two UGUSC		6.	ten GWGS
	× six GWGS	___		– three AJWH	___		+ five ALLM ___

7.	two AHUST		8.	six BFIH		9.	ten UGUSC
	× two AJWH	___		– four UGUSC ___			+ ten AHUST ___

10. eight TJSD
    – eight TJSD   ___

3. Have students check their papers as you read the answers:

1. ($48)	2. ($12)	3. ($480)
4. ($360)	5. ($40)	6. ($35)
7. ($800)	8. ($400)	9. ($600)
10. ($0)		

4. Have each student compose 5 money math problems and answer them.

Exercise 13: Millard Fillmore

1. Read to the class:

Vice President Millard Fillmore became president when Zachary Taylor died after being president for only 16 months. President Fillmore took over at a difficult time. The country was trying to decide whether to allow slavery in territories that were becoming states. Slaves are people who are owned by other people. President Taylor had supported steps to keep slavery from spreading into new states. President Fillmore was willing to *compromise*. That means he was willing to let slave owners have part of what they wanted and let people who were against slavery have part of what they wanted. The Compromise of 1850 didn't make either side totally happy, and Americans continued to argue about slavery.

In foreign affairs President Fillmore was more successful. He had U.S. Navy officer Commodore Perry sail some ships to Japan. A treaty of trade and friendship was signed between Japan and the United States. Millard Fillmore, after serving out the term of Zachary Taylor, wanted to get elected for his own 4-year term but he could not. Still, being president for over $2\frac{1}{2}$ years was quite an accomplishment for a boy who had gone to school only long enough to learn the alphabet. He later taught himself to read when he was a teenager learning how to make clothes for a living.

2. Have students copy the following:

   Millard Fillmore (1800–1874)

   Became president when President Zachary Taylor died

   Thirteenth president (1850–1853)

   Supported the Compromise of 1850

   Sent Commodore Matthew Perry to Japan to open trade

3. Have each student compose 3 sentences about Millard Fillmore and sketch a picture illustrating the sentences.

4. Have students read their sentences to the class and show their drawings.

Exercise 14: Franklin Pierce

1. Read to the class:

Franklin Pierce was very popular before he became president, but after he became president he became very unpopular. That's because he could not solve the argument over slavery. President Pierce thought it was a good idea to let new territories and new states decide for themselves whether or not they wanted to allow slavery. Fighting broke out in Kansas between people who wanted slavery and those who did not want slavery. President Pierce was not nominated to run for a second term. This was fine with his wife, who refused to live in Washington, D.C. Perhaps this was because the Pierces' 11-year-old son, Bennie, was killed in a train accident when the family was traveling to Washington, D.C. The Pierces' other 2 children had died earlier. Franklin Pierce had a problem with alcohol when he was a young man. He then stopped drinking and did not take a drink for 20 years. But 6 years after he stopped being president, his wife died. Then Franklin Pierce began to drink again. He drank heavily until he died 5 years later.

2. Have students copy the following:

   Franklin Pierce (1804–1869)

   Fourteenth president (1853–1857)

   Believed each state should be allowed to decide for itself whether or not to have slavery

   Fighting over slavery broke out in Kansas

   Was not chosen to run for a second term

   Had many family tragedies

3. Have each student compose 3 sentences about Franklin Pierce and sketch a picture illustrating the sentences.

4. Have students read their sentences to the class and show their drawings.

Exercise 15: James Buchanan

Read Aloud

1. Read to the class:

James Buchanan was the only president who never married. He was engaged to be married when he was a young man but his bride-to-be died suddenly. Without a wife, President Buchanan had his niece Harriet act as hostess at the White House, welcoming and entertaining guests. She was a very popular young lady who liked to dance. This was an activity her uncle didn't always approve of in the White House. President Buchanan could not solve the disagreement between southern and northern states over slavery. He sometimes seemed to be more on the side of the southern states. Two and a half months before his term of office ended, the state of South Carolina broke away from the United States. Abraham Lincoln had already been elected president but had not taken office. He would have to decide what to do about states that said they were no longer a part of the United States. As James Buchanan departed the White House he said to incoming President Abraham Lincoln, "If you are as happy, my dear sir, on entering this house as I am on leaving it and returning home, you are the happiest man in this country."

Write on Board

2. Have students copy the following:

James Buchanan (1791–1868)

Fifteenth president (1857–1861)

Niece served as First Lady

Could not solve the problem of slavery

South Carolina said it was no longer part of the U.S. during his term of office.

3. Have each student compose 3 sentences about James Buchanan and sketch a picture illustrating the sentences.

4. Have students read their sentences to the class and show their drawings.

Exercise 16: California

Read Aloud

1. Read to the class:

California was the home of many American Indian tribes. In 1769 a Catholic priest, Father Junipero Serra, accompanied a Spanish military expedition into California. The Spanish soldiers set up military forts and Father Serra established Catholic missions to convert the Indians to Christianity. Many California cities have the names of these Spanish missions. San Diego, Los Angeles, and San Francisco are some of them. Settlers from Mexico came to California and started large ranches where they raised cattle, horses, hogs, sheep, and goats. Americans came to California to trade and settle. In 1846 settlers in California *revolted against* Mexican rule. That means they tried to get rid of Mexican rule. The revolt became known as the "Bear Flag Revolt," because the flag they carried had a picture of a bear on it. When the U.S. won the Mexican War, California became a part of the United States in 1848. Gold was found that same year, and all kinds of people rushed to California in 1849 to try to get rich. California is called the *Golden State.* In 1850 it became the thirty-first state of the U.S.

2. Have students copy the following:

   California

   Spanish established military forts, missions, and ranches.

   Americans traded and settled.

   Bear Flag Revolt 1846

   U.S. defeated Mexico in war and California became a part of U.S. in 1848.

   Gold rush 1849

   Became the thirty-first state in 1850

3. Have each student compose 3 sentences about California and sketch a picture illustrating the sentences.

4. Have students read their sentences to the class and show their drawings.

Exercise 17: Water

1. Read to the class:

Earth is sometimes called *the blue planet* because most of its surface is covered by water. If you go out in space as the astronauts do and look down at the Earth, it will look like a ball, with most of it blue. We call the water in the air around us *humidity.* Your body is composed mostly of water. If you did not have any water to drink you might survive about 6 days. Without water, farms could not grow much of what we eat. Farm animals would die without water.

We store water in lakes and dams. To make water safe for drinking and home use we run it through a water treatment plant to take bad things out of it. Many places also put fluoride in drinking water to help prevent cavities in teeth.

Water is used to produce some of the electricity we use. Electricity produced by using falling water is called *hydroelectricity.* When you see *hydro* or *hydr* in the front of a word (prefix), the prefix usually comes from a Greek word meaning water. Thus, *hydroelectricity* means *water electricity.* Water is also used by many factories and businesses in making the products they sell.

2. Have students copy the following:

   Water

   Covers most of the Earth's surface

   Human body mostly water

   Makes farms and ranches possible

   Used to make electricity

   Used in making many things

3. Have each student compose 3 sentences about water and sketch a picture illustrating the sentences.

4. Have students read their sentences to the class and show their drawings.

Exercise 18: Oil

1. Read to the class:

You might think that oil is just dirty water, but it is something quite different. Oil doesn't come down from the clouds in the form of rain. It started out as dead animals and decaying plants that were buried in the Earth millions of years ago. Being buried all those years, it changed into a black liquid that we today call *oil* or *petroleum*. Oil wells are where long metal pipes are stuck down into the ground to get to pools of oil. The oil is pumped up and then sent to a refinery, a place that turns the oil into useful products. Oil is turned into gasolines that run automobiles, airplanes, lawn mowers, and countless other machines. Oil is also used to make plastic, which is used to make all kinds of other things. Your lunch box or jacket may be a product of oil. Nylon and polyester are called *petrochemicals.* Petrochemical products come from petroleum or natural gas. Depending on where you live and the type of heating system your home has, you may be heating with oil.

2. Have students copy the following:

   Oil (Petroleum)

   Started out millions of years ago as dead animals and decaying plants

   Goes from oil well to refinery

   Used to run all kinds of machines

   Turned into all kinds of products (petrochemical products)

3. Have each student compose 3 sentences about oil and sketch a picture illustrating the sentences.

4. Have students read their sentences to the class and show their drawings.

Exercise 19: Natural Gas

Read Aloud

1. Read to the class:

Natural gas, like oil, comes from wells that pump it up from beneath the ground. Like oil, it was formed in the Earth millions of years ago. As it is pumped up and sent by pipeline to a separation plant, it is a mixture of liquid and gases. The liquid and gases are then separated. The main gas is methane. Methane is piped directly to cities to be used as fuel for furnaces, hot water heaters, stoves, and other things. Other gases leave the separation plant in the forms of diesel, propane, butane, and ethane. Diesel powers school buses, big trucks, some family vehicles, as well as other things. Gas stations usually have some pumps labeled *diesel*. The pumps that aren't labeled diesel have the gasoline that other vehicles use. Propane tanks and butane tanks store fuel for many other uses. You may have seen a camping stove, lantern, or something else that uses propane or butane. Ethane is processed into ethylene, which is turned into all kinds of plastic products.

Write on Board

2. Have students copy the following:

   Natural Gas

   Formed millions of years ago from decaying animals and plants

   Pumped from wells and piped to a plant that separates it into liquid and gases

   Methane used in furnaces, stoves, hot water heaters, and other things

   Diesel used to power buses, trucks, some family vehicles, and other things

   Ethane turned into ethylene, which is turned into plastic products

3. Have each student compose 3 sentences about natural gas and sketch a picture illustrating the sentences.

4. Have students read their sentences to the class and show their drawings.

Exercise 20: Coal

Read Aloud

1. Read to the class:

Trees and plants died and started to decay millions of years ago in swampy forests. After a very long time being covered by dirt and rock, the decaying trees and plants hardened into a black rock that we call *coal*. It seems strange that a rock will burn, but coal does. Today you may never see a piece of coal, but less than 100 years ago most homes and schools were heated by furnaces that burned coal. If you had lived at that time your parents or guardians might have had you stoke the furnace. *Stoking the furnace* meant shoveling coal into the furnace and doing the necessary things to keep the furnace burning. Where did you get the coal? You would order the coal, and then a truck would pull up to your house and dump the amount of coal you had ordered. The coal was usually dumped down a chute to a place in the basement that was by the furnace. Coal is used today by many power plants to make the electricity we use. Coal is taken out of the ground and carried in trucks and train cars to power plants. It is burned to heat water to make steam. The steam turns a thing called a *turbine*, which is used to run a generator that generates electricity. The electricity is sent through power lines to homes and other buildings where we switch on lights, plug in vacuum cleaners, and watch TV. When your power goes off you know it. Coal is also very important in making steel.

2. Have students copy the following:

    Coal

    Formed millions of years ago from dying trees and plants

    Mined from the ground and taken to power plants

    Burned to heat water and steam

    Steam turns turbine that runs generator that generates electricity.

    Electricity sent to homes, buildings, and other places where electricity is needed.

    Coal also used in producing steel.

3. Have each student compose 3 sentences about coal and sketch a picture illustrating the sentences.

4. Have students read their sentences to the class and show their drawings.

Exercise 21: Abraham Lincoln

1. Read to the class:

When Abraham Lincoln was running for president in 1860, 11-year-old Grace Bedell wrote him a letter telling him he would look better with a beard. All pictures of Lincoln as president show him with a beard.

Lincoln was a Republican, and the Republican Party was against slavery. The southern states had slavery, and when Lincoln became president, most of them decided to quit the U.S. But President Lincoln would not let states quit the U.S. A big war called the *Civil War* broke out between the southern states that were trying to quit and the northern states that were trying to keep them from quitting. The war lasted 4 years. The North won the war, and the South had to give up owning slaves.

During the war Lincoln issued a written statement called *the Emancipation Proclamation*. It said that slaves in states that were fighting against the U.S. were free. After the war the Thirteenth Amendment to the U.S. Constitution was passed. The Thirteenth Amendment said there would be no slavery in the United States.

A few days after the war ended, John Wilkes Booth, a man who was unhappy that the North had won, shot and killed Abraham Lincoln while he and Mrs. Lincoln were attending a play.

2. Have students copy the following:

Abraham Lincoln (1809–1865)

Sixteenth president (1861–1865)

Would not let southern states secede (quit the U.S.)

North won the Civil War and South gave up slavery.

Lincoln assassinated (killed) by John Wilkes Booth

Thirteenth Amendment to the U.S. Constitution said there would be no slavery in the U.S.

3. Have each student compose 3 sentences about Abraham Lincoln and sketch a picture illustrating the sentences.

4. Have students read their sentences to the class and show their drawings.

Exercise 22: Andrew Johnson

1. Read to the class:

When President Lincoln was shot and killed in 1865, Vice President Andrew Johnson became president. From a poor family, Andrew Johnson had never attended school. While learning to become a maker of clothes, Johnson had heard others read aloud from books and decided he wanted to know how to read. He taught himself to read by staying up late at night and studying books. At age 15 he left home, and by the time he was 18 he opened his own tailor shop. His 16-year-old wife taught him how to write.

Johnson was elected to many political jobs. He was elected as President Lincoln's vice president when Lincoln was elected to a second term. Lincoln liked Johnson because during the Civil War he stayed loyal to the United States when many other southerners did not. After the North won the Civil War, President Johnson did not want to punish the South as many northerners in Congress did. He also did not want former slaves to have the same rights as white southerners. But the Republicans did, and they controlled Congress. Republicans in Congress also tried to keep southerners who had been in high positions in the South from coming back into Congress. Congress tried to remove Andrew Johnson from office by impeachment for firing Secretary of War Edwin Stanton. The vote to remove President Johnson failed by 1 vote. After completing Abraham Lincoln's term of office as president, Andrew Johnson returned to his home state of Tennessee. He eventually managed to get himself elected to the U.S. Senate shortly before he died.

2. Have students copy the following:

Andrew Johnson (1808–1875)

Seventeenth president (1865–1869)

Southerner who stayed loyal to the U.S. during the Civil War

Became president when Lincoln assassinated

Did not want to punish the South or give blacks equal rights

Congress tried to remove him from office, but failed to do so by 1 vote.

3. Have each student compose 3 sentences about Andrew Johnson and sketch a picture illustrating the sentences.

4. Have students read their sentences to the class and show their drawings.

Exercise 23: Ulysses Simpson Grant

1. Read to the class:

When 17-year-old Hiram Ulysses Grant went away to college at West Point a mistake was made in listing his name. They listed him as "Ulysses Simpson" and from then on he became "Ulysses Simpson Grant." West Point trains students to be military officers. In 1839 when Grant entered West Point, horses were very important to the army; automobiles had not yet been invented. Grant loved horses and he became the best rider in the college. He graduated at the age of 21 and proved to be a very good army officer. He served with distinction during the Mexican War from 1846 to 1848.

After the war he was sent out west but did not like being away from his wife. Five years after the Mexican War he resigned his commission. As a civilian he had a very hard time earning a living for his wife and growing family. He tried farming and selling wood. When the Civil War came along in 1861 he was happy to leave his job as a clerk in his father's leather goods store and go back into the army. He was so good at being a soldier that by the end of the war in 1865 he was in charge of the entire Union army that won the Civil War.

A very popular Grant won the presidential election of 1868 and was sworn in as president in 1869. In only 8 years he had gone from store clerk to president of the United States. He served 2 terms as president, but most people who study history do not think he was as good a president as he had been a general. Some of the men he appointed to office turned out to be dishonest.

After being president he lost money investing in businesses. The author Mark Twain was a friend of Grant's and encouraged him to write a book about his life. Grant needed money, so he decided to write the book. Four days after completing the book, he died of throat cancer. He had been a smoker of about 20 cigars a day for many years. Much of the book was written while he was in extreme pain from the cancer. The book made his widow rich.

2. Have students copy the following:

Ulysses Simpson Grant (1822–1885)

West Point Military Academy graduate

Commanding general of the Union Army

Eighteenth president (1869–1877)

Autobiography made Grant's widow wealthy

3. Have each student compose 3 sentences about Ulysses Grant and sketch a picture illustrating the sentences.

4. Have students read their sentences to the class and show their drawings.

Exercise 24: Gettysburg

 Read Aloud

1. Read to the class:

Near the little town of Gettysburg, Pennsylvania, over 50,000 men were killed, wounded, or missing in a 3-day battle between northern and southern soldiers in the Civil War. General George Meade was in command of the Union troops and General Robert E. Lee commanded the Confederate troops. On the third day of the battle General Lee made a bad mistake by having a large part of his army, which was under the command of General George Pickett, attack the center of the Union line. Pickett's soldiers charged and were slaughtered. Lee lost the battle and retreated south with his remaining soldiers. The Civil War had been going on for 2 years and it would go on for 2 more years, but the battle of Gettysburg on July 1, 2, and 3 of 1863 was a turning point. The South would never again be strong enough to win the war. Because there were so many dead people to bury after the battle, a huge cemetery of soldiers' graves was soon in existence. President Abraham Lincoln went to the cemetery on November 19, 1863, to say a few words of respect in honor of those who had died in the tremendous battle. His short speech, known as *the Gettysburg Address,* ended with the words "... we here highly resolve that these dead shall not have died in vain; that this nation, under God, shall have a new birth of freedom, and that government of the people, by the people, for the people, shall not perish from the Earth."

 Write on Board

2. Have students copy the following:

   Battle of Gettysburg (July 1, 2, 3, 1863)

   Over 50,000 casualties

   Turned the Civil War in favor of the North

   Lincoln's Gettysburg Address (November 19, 1863)

   Gettysburg Address honored dead soldiers and freedom.

3. Have each student compose 3 sentences about Gettysburg and sketch a picture illustrating the sentences.

4. Have students read their sentences to the class and show their drawings.

Chapter Six

Fourth Grade Lesson Plans

Exercise 1: Flowers

 Read Aloud 1. Read to the class:

There are over 250,000 species of flowering plants on Earth. Some flowers are *annuals,* meaning they die each year and must be started over from seeds they have produced and dropped on the ground. Other flowers are *perennials,* meaning that they come up more than 1 year, sometimes for many years, without dying and starting from new seed. Perennials store food in their root systems underground, sometimes in bulbs. When the temperature, sun, and soil conditions are right, perennials are all set to pop up again. To produce seeds, flowers have to be pollinated. When bees buzz from flower to flower, they unintentionally carry pollen that will fertilize the other plant and cause it to produce seeds. Wind blows pollen from plant to plant and sometimes that causes our eyes to water and our nose to run, and we sneeze. We call this condition an *allergy.*

 Write on Board 2. Have students copy the following:

Flowers

Annuals start from new seed each year.

Perennials survive more than 1 year.

To produce seeds, a flower must be pollinated.

Bees and wind are two ways of pollinating flowers.

Blowing pollen is a cause for some people's allergies.

3. Have students copy the following and give them 5 to 10 minutes to write an answer:

Would the world be a better place without flowers?

Why or why not?

4. Have students read and discuss their answers or draw a picture about flowers or do both.

Exercise 2: Trees

 1. Read to the class:

Some trees are like flowers in that they develop buds and bloom. The famous cherry trees in Washington, D.C., are an example. Apples, oranges, peaches, and other kinds of fruit come from fruit trees. Some trees produce nuts. Walnut trees and pecan trees are examples of nut-producing trees. There are many types of trees that do not produce fruit. Some trees have leaves that change color with the seasons and fall off. Other trees do not. In general, trees are divided into two main types: deciduous trees, which shed their leaves every year, and coniferous trees, which do not shed their leaves. Cottonwoods, common along riverbanks in prairie states of the U.S., are deciduous. Pine trees, common in the Rocky Mountains, are coniferous. High in the Rocky Mountains you will reach the *tree line,* which is where the trees stop. Above the tree line the conditions for growing trees are not favorable. Wind, unmelted snow, rocky soil, and cold temperatures combine to keep trees from growing.

When a lot of trees are growing near each other it is called a *forest.* Some areas of the world, like the tropical rain forest in the Amazon River region of South America, are so hot and get so much rain that the trees grow very fast to reach up to the rays of the equatorial sun. The tropical rain forests in South America, in Africa, and in regions between Asia and Australia, are home to a great many birds, animals, and plants, as well as snakes, ants, and all kinds of insects and other creatures that we humans find unpleasant and dangerous. Some trees live for hundreds, even thousands of years, so there are places where forests are quite old. Many forests have been cut down at one time or another, so they are not very old. When replanted, forests grow back. This makes trees a renewable resource.

 2. Have students copy the following:

Trees

Some trees produce fruit or nuts.

Deciduous trees shed leaves each year.

Coniferous trees do not shed leaves each year.

Forests are places where a lot of trees grow.

Some trees can live as long as thousands of years.

Trees are a renewable resource.

3. Have students copy the following and give them 5 to 10 minutes to write an answer: What are trees used for and should they be used that way?

4. Have students read and discuss their answers or draw a picture about trees or do both.

Exercise 3: Fish

1. Read to the class:

One of the unusual things about fish compared to humans is that they can breathe underwater. This is possible because they have gills instead of lungs. Both gills and lungs are for the purpose of getting oxygen. Both air and water contain oxygen, although air has much more of it. We breathe in air, separate the oxygen from carbon dioxide in our lungs, and breathe out the carbon dioxide. Blood sends the oxygen to cells in our body. Fish use gills, which are located behind the head, to separate the oxygen and carbon dioxide. Water is taken in through the mouth of a fish and washed over the gills, which separate the oxygen in the water from the carbon dioxide in the water. The fish keeps the oxygen and gets rid of the carbon dioxide. The carbon dioxide is washed out in the water that is sent out of the fish's body through the slit or slits on the sides of the gills. People cannot breathe properly underwater and a fish cannot breathe properly when it is not in water. When a fish is out of water, it makes a futile effort to take in water through the mouth, take out the oxygen with its gills, and send the nonexistent water out through the slit or slits on its side. It is in effect what we humans would call "gasping for air" and "suffocating," but for the fish it is "gasping for water" and "suffocating."

Most fish can swim faster than humans, and some fish can swim much faster than humans. An average human swimmer can swim about 4 miles per hour for a short distance. A marlin, which is a popular fish that people fish for in the ocean, can swim 50 miles per hour. *Flying fish* can burst out of the water and glide 330 feet in the air. The porcupine fish protects itself by gulping so much water that it swells up to where its spines stick out in porcupine fashion. Swelling up like a balloon, with sharp little needlelike things sticking out all over its body, it can't swim very fast to get away from predators, but what other fish wants to swallow a ball of needles? There are over 21,000 species of fish, with some very unusual differences among them.

2. Have students copy the following:

Fish

Fish have gills instead of lungs.

Fish take in water through the mouth and the water washes over the gills.

The gills keep the oxygen.

The water, containing carbon dioxide, leaves the fish through a slit or slits on the sides of the gills.

3. Have students copy the following and give them 5 to 10 minutes to write an answer:

   What things do you think fish would find unusual about us and why would they find them unusual?

4. Have students read and discuss their answers or draw a picture about fish or do both.

Exercise 4: Birds

1. Read to the class:

A bird's body is designed for flight, although there are some species of birds that have lost the ability to fly. A bird's body has a light skeleton and is streamlined to cut through the air. A bird uses its wings to push downward and backward to give it *lift* into the air. The wings almost touch each other when they are at the top of their stroke before starting down again. The wings are spread out away from the body so that the bird can glide as effortlessly as you might coast on a bicycle. The 9,000 species of birds on Earth are the only creatures that have feathers. Most birds get rid of their feathers once or twice a year, and they grow a new set each time they *molt*. The beaks of birds vary considerably according to what they use them for. Some species have long thin beaks. Other species have a broad beak that curves back underneath. Birds have no teeth to chew food with, so the food is ground up inside the bird's body in a *gizzard*. Baby birds hatch out of eggs that the mother, or sometimes the father, *incubates* by sitting on them. Some birds migrate many miles, going from place to place during different seasons of the year. Many birds have keenly developed eyesight. While flying high they can spot a small animal, a fish, or something else that appeals to their appetite. They swoop down from the sky so fast that their prey is often unaware that they are about to become bird food. Some birds have a life span of only a year. Others may live 60 years or longer.

2. Have students copy the following:

   Birds

   Their bodies are designed for flying.

   There are 9,000 species of birds.

   Birds are the only creatures that have feathers.

   Birds have no teeth, but a gizzard inside their bodies grinds up food.

   Baby birds hatch from eggs that are incubated.

3. Have students copy the following and give them 5 to 10 minutes to write an answer:

   Explain what you think it would be like to be a bird.

4. Have students read and discuss their answers or draw a picture about birds or do both.

Exercise 5: Rutherford B. Hayes

Read Aloud

1. Read to the class:

Rutherford B. Hayes won one of the most disputed elections in American history. In November 1876 Americans voted for president. When the vice president was supposed to announce the winner of the election to members of the U.S. Senate he could not because Florida, Louisiana, and South Carolina each had 2 different sets of electoral votes. One set of electoral votes, if accepted, would make Republican Rutherford B. Hayes the winner. If the other set of electoral votes was accepted, Democrat Samuel J. Tilden would be president. Republicans and Democrats in Congress disagreed and argued over who should be president. After several months an election commission that had been appointed to settle the dispute announced that Hayes was the winner.

Some people thought that the disagreeing sides had made a deal. Hayes would get to become president and U.S. Army troops would leave the South. U.S. Army troops had been stationed in southern states since the end of the Civil War to make sure that southern states did what Congress wanted. This was known as *Reconstruction.* Congress wanted to make sure that southern states did not go back to the way things had been before the Civil War. White southerners thought it was unfair to have U.S. Army soldiers treating the South like it was an occupied country. Congress thought it was necessary to have U.S. soldiers in the South to ensure that blacks and whites had equal rights. Hayes became president and U.S. Army troops left the South. Blacks were no longer slaves, but southern states brought in segregation. Whites and blacks had separate schools, separate drinking fountains, separate places to sit in movie theaters, restaurants, buses, and other places. Segregation continued until the 1960s.

Rutherford B. Hayes was an honest and fair president who angered many politicians by trying to get rid of the dishonest practices in government. He read the Bible and had prayers every morning before starting work. His wife was the first president's wife who was a college graduate. She became known as "Lemonade Lucy" because she would not allow alcohol to be served in the White House. She was a very popular First Lady, probably the most popular since Dolley Madison, the wife of President James Madison. Rutherford B. Hayes did not run for a second term, keeping the promise he had made that if elected he would serve only 1 term.

Write on Board

2. Have students copy the following:

Rutherford B. Hayes (1822–1893)

Nineteenth president (1877–1881)

Hayes won a very disputed presidential election over Samuel J. Tilden.

When he became president U.S. soldiers left the South, ending "Reconstruction."

Hayes tried to be fair and end dishonest activities in government.

Lucy Hayes was the first president's wife to have a college degree.

3. Have students copy the following and give them 5 to 10 minutes to write an answer: Why is it important for people in government to be honest?

4. Have students read and discuss their answers or draw a picture about Rutherford B. Hayes or do both.

Exercise 6: James Garfield and Chester Alan Arthur

1. Read to the class:

In the year 1881 there were 3 different presidents. Rutherford B. Hayes was president until the newly elected president, James Garfield, took over on March 4. President Garfield was shot on July 2, 1881, and did not recover, finally dying on September 19, 1881. Then Vice President Chester Alan Arthur became president.

The presidencies of Hayes, Garfield, and Arthur were all greatly affected by the way people got government jobs. "To the victor belong the spoils" is an old saying that means whoever wins at something gets whatever rewards there are for winning. From the time of President Andrew Jackson until the time of President Hayes, government jobs were rewards to people who supported the person who won the election. This was known as the *spoils system*. When Rutherford B. Hayes became president he thought that some jobs should go to people on the basis of their ability, rather than merely because they had helped elect him. One of the people President Hayes, a Republican, fired from a government job because he thought he wasn't doing a good job was Chester Alan Arthur, also a Republican. Chester Alan Arthur, before being fired, was in charge of collecting taxes on goods shipped into the port at New York City.

When President Hayes left office, the new president, James Garfield, tried to follow the policy of Hayes in awarding some government jobs on the basis of ability. A man named Charles Julius Guiteau, who did not get a government job and thought he deserved one, used a handgun to shoot President Garfield when he was at a train station.

Chester Alan Arthur had been elected as Garfield's vice president and when Garfield died he became president. Everyone expected President Arthur to go back to the spoils system. But Chester Alan Arthur surprised people by working hard and trying to be the best president he could be. He signed into law the Pendleton Act of 1883, which is still the basis of how many government jobs are awarded. The president still appoints people to high government jobs, like the president's cabinet, but people take tests to get other jobs. Working for the government is called *civil service*. Someday, if you want to work for the government, you may take a civil service test to try to get a job.

A year and a half after leaving office, Chester Alan Arthur died. Shortly before he died he had all of his private papers and records burned. Some people think he did this to cover up bad things he had done before becoming president. He wanted people to remember that he had tried to be a good president, rather than remembering the things he had done before becoming president.

2. Have students copy the following:

James Garfield (1831–1881) and Chester Alan Arthur (1830–1886)

James Garfield was the twentieth president (March 4, 1881–September 19, 1881).

Chester Alan Arthur was the twenty-first president (September 20, 1881–March 3, 1885).

Presidents Hayes, Garfield, and Arthur worked to get rid of the spoils system.

The Pendleton Act of 1883 became the basis for people to take tests to get government jobs.

3. Have students copy the following and give them 5 to 10 minutes to write an answer:

List 3 jobs that you think might be government jobs and tell what things you might need to know to do each of the jobs.

4. Have students read and discuss their answers or draw a picture about James Garfield or Chester Alan Arthur or do both.

Exercise 7: Grover Cleveland

1. Read to the class:

Grover Cleveland was 47 years old and a bachelor when he became the twenty-second president in 1885. Every president from March 4, 1861, until March 4, 1913, was a Republican except for Grover Cleveland, who was a Democrat. At the age of 49, President Cleveland married 21-year-old Frances Folson. When Frances Folson was 12 her father had died and Grover Cleveland, her father's law partner, had taken over her financial support. The wedding ceremony took place on June 2, 1886, in the Blue Room of the White House with a small group of family members and invited guests. The Marine Band, under the direction of John Philip Sousa, played the wedding march. Following the exchange of vows there was dancing in the East Room and a wedding banquet in the State Dining Room. The couple had 5 children during a 22-year marriage that ended when Grover Cleveland died in 1908 at the age of 71.

Grover Cleveland was the only president to be elected to a 4-year term of office, get defeated for reelection, and then, 4 years later, win election again after somebody else had been president. Grover Cleveland therefore became our twenty-second president and our twenty-fourth president, being president both before and after President Benjamin Harrison. President Cleveland's terms of office were marked by battles with Congress. President Cleveland vetoed 584 bills of Congress. President Cleveland vetoed far more bills than any other president except President Franklin Roosevelt, who vetoed 635 bills during 12 years of being president from 1933 to 1945.

President Cleveland had been a smoker for many years and during his second term in office developed cancer in his mouth. He didn't want to alarm the country so he pretended to go on vacation and had surgery performed onboard a ship. Several weeks after the first surgery to cut out the cancer he had another secret operation onboard ship that finished removing the cancer and gave him an artificial upper left jaw made out of rubber.

Cleveland became very unpopular during his second term, perhaps in part because he had lost a lot of weight following the operations and was irritable because of the rubber jaw. Some accused him of being a "dictator" when he had soldiers break up striking train workers to ensure public safety and keep the mail from being stopped. In addition, there was a depression, which means that a lot of people had no jobs. A bunch of unemployed men went to Washington, D.C., and their leader Jacob Coxey wanted the government to spend money on projects to give them jobs. President Cleveland had the police and the National Guard run the men off. President Cleveland was probably very happy to end his second term of office and go on hunting trips with his buddies, which was something he really liked to do.

2. Have students copy the following:

   Grover Cleveland (1837–1908)

   Twenty-second president (1885–1889)

   Twenty-fourth president (1893–1897)

   President Cleveland vetoed 584 bills of Congress and only 7 vetoes were overridden.

   Cleveland had secret operations to cut out cancer and put in an artificial upper left jaw.

   An economic depression and unemployment made President Cleveland unpopular by the end of his second term of office.

3. Have students copy the following and give them 5 to 10 minutes to write an answer:

   Should a president's medical condition be made known to the public? Why or why not?

4. Have students read and discuss their answers or draw a picture about Grover Cleveland or do both.

Exercise 8: Benjamin Harrison

1. Read to the class:

President Benjamin Harrison was the grandson of President William Henry Harrison. Although Benjamin Harrison had a famous grandfather, he was determined all his life to be successful because he earned it rather than because of his family name. After graduating from college he became a hard-working lawyer. During the Civil War he worked his way up from captain to brigadier general, fighting in more battles than his grandfather had when he was a famous general years earlier. After the Civil War Benjamin Harrison went back to practicing law and eventually served a 6-year term as a U.S. senator from Indiana.

When Benjamin Harrison became president in 1889 his personality didn't seem to fit the job. He was quiet and thoughtful and preferred being left alone. In those days ordinary people could visit the president without being invited. Presidents would usually set aside a couple of hours or more each day when citizens could drop in for a few minutes to tell the president their troubles, ask for a government job or help of some kind, or whatever. The White House grounds were usually open to the public and visitors sat or stood on the grass while children ran around in play. Sometimes people picnicked. Some visitors were rude enough to stop their horse-drawn carriages on the driveway in front of the White House and try to peer through the window into the private dining room to watch the president and his family eating. Benjamin Harrison withdrew from the public as much as the job of the president would permit. When he went for a walk he would try not to look directly at people so that he could ignore them when they said hello.

While Benjamin Harrison was running for a second term of office, his wife Caroline became very ill. He sat up late by her bedside, sometimes spending the whole night sitting there. She died from tuberculosis 2 weeks before the election. Benjamin Harrison lost the election, which was probably just as well because he didn't seem to like the job of being president much anyway. Three years after leaving the office of president, the 62-year-old Benjamin Harrison married the 37-year-old widowed niece of his deceased wife. His 41-year-old son and his 38-year-old daughter didn't approve of the marriage and they wouldn't have anything to do with their father from then on. Benjamin Harrison and Mary were married almost 5 years until he died in 1901 at the age of 67.

2. Have students copy the following:

Benjamin Harrison (1833–1901)

Twenty-third president (1889–1893)

Benjamin Harrison was the grandson of President William Henry Harrison.

Benjamin Harrison didn't care for all of the seeing and meeting people that a president has to do.

Benjamin Harrison became president by defeating President Grover Cleveland.

Grover Cleveland came back 4 years after being president once to become president again by defeating President Benjamin Harrison.

3. Have students copy the following and give them 5 to 10 minutes to write an answer:

Would it be a good idea for presidents today to set aside a couple of hours each day for ordinary people to drop by and visit with them? Why or why not?

4. Have students read and discuss their answers or draw a picture about Benjamin Harrison or do both.

Exercise 9: Roman Numerals: I–XXX

1. Say to the class:

    "When we write numbers today we practically always use what are called *Arabic numerals.* They are called *Arabic* because we got them hundreds of years ago from the Arabs, who got them hundreds of years before that from people living in India. We also sometimes use *Roman numerals.* Roman numerals were passed down to us from Ancient Rome, where they were used centuries ago. Roman numerals are often used in making outlines and sometimes to separate chapters in books or parts of legal documents. You will sometimes see Roman numerals used for the main parts of the U.S. Constitution. I am going to write some Roman numerals on the board, along with their Arabic counterparts, and I want you to copy both."

2. Have students copy the following:

I: 1	XI: 11	XXI: 21
II: 2	XII: 12	XXII: 22
III: 3	XIII: 13	XXIII: 23
IV: 4	XIV: 14	XXIV: 24
V: 5	XV: 15	XXV: 25
VI: 6	XVI: 16	XXVI: 26
VII: 7	XVII: 17	XXVII: 27
VIII: 8	XVIII: 18	XXVIII: 28
IX: 9	XIX: 19	XXIX: 29
X: 10	XX: 20	XXX: 30

3. Have students copy the following and give them 5 to 10 minutes to write an answer:

    Do you think it would be easier, about the same, or harder to do math problems using Roman numerals rather than Arabic numerals? Why?

4. Have students read their answers to the class and discuss or have individual students come up to the board and write from memory whatever Roman numeral you ask them to write or have them do both.

Exercise 10: Roman Numerals: Converting to Arabic

1. Say to the class: "The Arabic system of numbering, which we use most of the time, consist of 10 numbers. Copy them as I write them on the board: 0, 1, 2, 3, 4, 5, 6, 7, 8, 9."

2. Say to the class: "To make larger numbers using Arabic numerals, we merely combine numbers to create whatever number we want. Here are a few examples for you to copy."

3. Write on the board and have students copy the following:

   4, 49, 498, 4,984, 49,984

4. Say to the class: "The Roman system of numbering, which we occasionally use, consists of 7 numbers. Copy them as I write them on the board with their Arabic counterparts."

5. Write on the board and have students copy the following:

   I: 1, V: 5, X: 10, L: 50, C: 100, D: 500, M: 1000.

6. Say to the class: "When we use Roman numerals, we make larger or smaller numbers according to which side of the number the smaller number is placed. If the smaller number is placed on the right of the larger number, the smaller number is added to the larger number. If the smaller number is placed to the left of the larger number, the smaller number is subtracted from the larger number. Here are a few examples for you to copy."

7. Write on the board and have students copy the following:

   V: 5, IV: 4, VI: 6, X: 10, XI: 11, IX: 9,

   L: 50, XL: 40, LX: 60, C: 100, CI: 101, IC: 99.

8. Say to the class: "I am going to write 20 Roman numbers on the board. I want you to copy them and write the Arabic equivalent for each."

9. Write the Roman number on the board, *but leave out* the Arabic equivalents shown here in parentheses:

1. C (100)	11. IVC (96)
2. MC (1100)	12. VIII (8)
3. II (2)	13. XL (40)
4. XX (20)	14. IL (49)
5. XXXI (31)	15. XC (90)
6. IX (9)	16. CCL (250)
7. XXIX (29)	17. LCC (150)
8. CM (900)	18. DC (600)
9. IC (99)	19. CIV (104)
10. CD (400)	20. MMVIII (2008)

10. As each student finishes have the student pair up and help a student who is not finished. When all students have finished, have them check their papers as you read the correct answers or put the correct answers on the board.

Exercise 11: Roman Numerals: Addition

 1. Write on the board and have the students copy the following:

I: 1	XXX: 30
II: 2	XL: 40
III: 3	L: 50
IV: 4	LX: 60
V: 5	XC: 90
VI: 6	C: 100
VII: 7	CC: 200
VIII: 8	CD: 400
IX: 9	D: 500
X: 10	CM: 900
XI: 11	M: 1000
XIX: 19	MM: 2000
XX: 20	

2. Say to the students: "I am going to put some addition problems on the board. The problems are going to be written in Roman numerals. You are to copy the problems as they are, put in the Arabic equivalent numbers, work the problems in Arabic, and then also write the answers in Roman numerals. I will work the first 2 problems with you to show you what I mean."

3. Write the following problems on the board, listing the Roman numerals but *leaving out* the Arabic numerals and the answers except for the first 2 problems, which you will complete for the students:

1.	I 1	2.	XL 40	3.	XX 20	4.	VI 6
	+ III 3		+ L 50		+ XXX 30		+ II 2
	IV 4		XC 90		L 50		VIII 8

5.	IX 9	6.	CC 200	7.	XXX 30	8.	CD 400
	+ X 10		+ CC 200		+ XXX 30		+ D 500
	XIX 19		CD 400		LX 60		CM 900

9.	VII 7	10.	M 1000	11.	D 500	12.	IV 4
	+ III 3		+ M 1000		+ D 500		+ V 5
	X 10		MM 2000		M 1000		IX 9

13.	XXX 30	14.	III 3	15.	XI 11	16.	CC 200
	+ LX 60		+ IV 4		+ VIII 8		CC 200
	XC 90		VII 7		XIX 19		+ D 500
							CM 900

17.	XC 90	18.	VIII 8	19.	XIX 19	20.	M 1000
	+ LX 60		+ VII 7		+ XI 11		+ CM 900
	+ L 50		+ V 5		+ XL 40		+ C 100
	CC 200		XX 20		LXX 70		MM 2000

4. As each student finishes, have the student pair up and help a student who has not finished. When all students have finished, have them check their papers as you read the correct answers or put the correct answers on the board.

Exercise 12: Roman Numerals: Subtraction

1. Write on the board and have the students copy the following:

I: 1	XX: 20
II: 2	XXX: 30
III: 3	XL: 40
IV: 4	L: 50
V: 5	LX: 60
VI: 6	XC: 90
VII: 7	C: 100
VIII: 8	CC: 200
IX: 9	CD: 400
X: 10	D: 500
XI: 11	CM: 900
XIX: 19	M: 1000
	MM: 2000

2. Say to the students: "I am going to put some subtraction problems on the board. The problems are going to be written in Roman numerals. You are to copy the problems as they are, put in the Arabic equivalent numbers, work the problems in Arabic, and then also write the answers in Roman numerals. I will work the first two problems with you to show you what I mean."

3. Write the following problems on the board, listing the Roman numerals and *leaving out* the Arabic numerals and the answers except for problems 1 and 2, which you will complete for the students:

1. III 3 – II 2 I 1	2. L 50 – XL 40 X 10	3. XXX 30 – XX 20 X 10	4. VIII 8 – VI 6 II 2
5. X 10 – IX 9 I 1	6. CC 200 – C 100 C 100	7. LX 60 – XXX 30 XXX 30	8. D 500 – CD 400 C 100
9. VII 7 – III 3 IV 4	10. MM 2000 – M 1000 M 1000	11. M 1000 – D 500 D 500	12. V 5 – IV 4 I 1
13. XC 90 – LX 60 XXX 30	14. IV 4 – III 3 I 1	15. XI 11 – VIII 8 III 3	16. CM 900 – D 500 CD 400
17. LX 60 – L 50 X 10	18. VIII 8 – V 5 III 3	19. LX 60 – XL 40 XX 20	20. M 1000 – CM 900 C 100

4. As each student finishes, have the student pair up and help a student who has not finished. When all students have finished, have them check their papers as you read the correct answers or put the correct answers on the board.

Exercise 13: William McKinley

1. Read to the class:

Eighteen-year-old William McKinley joined the Union Army as a private in 1861 to fight in the Civil War. Four years later he was discharged with the rank of captain, having been a brevet (honorary) major for the last 3 months of his military service. He became a lawyer and years later, in 1897, president.

Cuba had been a colony of Spain for a long time and the Cubans revolted, trying to get independence from Spain. A United States battleship, the USS *Maine*, blew up in a harbor at Havana, Cuba. The U.S. blamed Spain, and President McKinley asked Congress to declare war on Spain. The U.S. won the Spanish-American War in less than 4 months, and Spain turned over to the United States Cuba, Guam, Puerto Rico, and the Philippines. Puerto Rico and Guam became and still are U.S. territories. Cuba quickly became a country. The Philippines became a country on July 4, 1946, when the U.S. gave the Philippines independence.

Early in his second term of office President McKinley was assassinated by a man who fired 2 shots from a pistol as the president was shaking hands with people in a crowd at a fair. William McKinley had always been very concerned about his wife, who had epilepsy. He told those who were attending him after he had been shot, "My wife—be careful how you tell her." He died 8 days later and his last words were "Goodbye. Goodbye to all. It is God's will. His will, not ours, be done."

2. Have students copy the following:

    William McKinley (1843–1901)

    Twenty-fifth president (1897–1901)

    William McKinley was president during the Spanish-American War (1898).

    The U.S. won the war and got Cuba, Guam, Puerto Rico, and the Philippines.

    Guam and Puerto Rico remain U.S. territories, but we gave Cuba and the Philippines their independence long ago.

    President McKinley was the third American president to be assassinated.

3. Have students copy the following and give them 5 to 10 minutes to write an answer:

    Should Puerto Rico and Guam become states, remain territories, or become independent countries? Why?

4. Have students read and discuss their answers or draw a picture about William McKinley or do both.

Exercise 14: Theodore Roosevelt

1. Read to the class:

Theodore Roosevelt did everything with vigor. A sickly boy, troubled by asthma and other physical problems, he followed the advice of his father to build his body up and become strong. Lifting weights, hiking, boxing, and participating in various sports, Theodore Roosevelt became a champion of physical fitness and continued to pursue strenuous activities until the end of his life. He needed to be physically, mentally, and emotionally strong to overcome the tragedies and challenges he would face. When Theodore Roosevelt was 25 years old, his wife of 3 years and his mother died on the same day. To overcome his sorrow he left his home state of New York and went west to the Dakota Territory and became a rancher. He returned to New York 2 years later, remarried, and went back into politics. When the Spanish-American War came along in 1898, he recruited his own regiment of volunteers, known as the *Rough Riders,* and went off to fight in Cuba. Returning from the war a hero, he was elected vice president of the United States.

When President McKinley was assassinated, Theodore Roosevelt became the youngest president ever, at age 42. He was a popular and vigorous president. He brought under control big businesses that he thought were treating the public unfairly. He signed laws to create national parks. For settling a war between Russia and Japan he earned a Nobel Peace Prize. He got the United States to undertake the huge task of building the Panama Canal. He was the first president to ride in an automobile and the first president to ride in an airplane. He was the first president to go on a visit outside of the United States while serving as president, going to Panama to see how the construction of the canal was coming along. Before dying at the age of 60 Theodore Roosevelt was saddened by the death of one of his sons whose plane was shot down in 1918 during aerial combat in World War I. Two of his other sons died in World War II, 1 in Alaska in 1943 and the other in 1944, several days after making the D-Day landing at Normandy, France.

2. Have students copy the following:

   Theodore Roosevelt (1858–1919)

   Twenty-sixth president (1901–1909)

   He was a strong advocate of vigorous and active living.

   He became a hero in the Spanish-American War.

   As president, he regulated big businesses and set aside land for national parks.

   He got the United States to build the Panama Canal.

3. Have students copy the following and give them 5 to 10 minutes to write an answer:

   Why do you think the United States wanted a canal in Panama and why was it difficult to build?

4. Have students read their answers to the class and discuss or draw a picture about Theodore Roosevelt or do both.

Exercise 15: William Howard Taft

1. Read to the class:

Friends can sometimes be direct opposites in many ways. Such was the case of Theodore Roosevelt and William Howard Taft, who became good friends and then bitter enemies. Roosevelt was always on the go and thought a hunting trip was wonderful. Taft preferred more sedate activities and felt that a nap on the couch was better than any hunting trip. Yet the two enjoyed talking, joking around, and having a great time being together. President Theodore Roosevelt appointed William Howard Taft Secretary of War; today that position is called Secretary of Defense. When Theodore Roosevelt neared the end of his time in office he let everyone know that he thought his good friend William Howard Taft should be the next president.

Taft was nominated by the Republicans in 1908 and won the election. Roosevelt went happily off to Africa on a hunting trip. When Roosevelt came back from Africa he didn't like the way Taft was handling the job of president. Roosevelt had always been extremely forceful as president, thinking that a president could do anything that the U.S. Constitution did not forbid him from doing. Taft, on the other hand, thought a president should only do those things that the U.S. Constitution actually stated a president could do. Roosevelt continued to criticize Taft and then decided he would run for office again and replace Taft as president. Roosevelt and Taft split the Republican Party apart in the 1912 election, and Democrat Woodrow Wilson was elected president. Roosevelt came in second and Taft was third.

Roosevelt and Taft never renewed their friendship. Taft became a professor of law at Yale University and then chief justice of the U.S. Supreme Court. In a job better suited to his nature, Taft lost about 100 of the more than 350 pounds he had ballooned to as president. While Taft was president an oversized bathtub was installed in the White House. Taft was very happy being the chief justice of the U.S. Supreme Court because it was a job he had always wanted. His wife and good friend Theodore Roosevelt had encouraged him to run for president in 1908, but he really hadn't wanted to do it.

2. Have students copy the following:

   William Howard Taft (1857–1930)

   Twenty-seventh president (1909–1913)

   Theodore Roosevelt didn't like the way Taft was doing the job of president.

   Roosevelt and Taft spilt the Republican Party in the 1912 election, and Democrat Woodrow Wilson won the election.

   Taft was chief justice of the U.S. Supreme Court from 1921 to 1930.

3. Have students copy the following and give them 5 to 10 minutes to write an answer:

   Who was a better friend, Theodore Roosevelt or William Howard Taft? Why do you think so?

4. Have students read their answers to the class and discuss or draw a picture about William Howard Taft or do both.

Exercise 16: Woodrow Wilson

1. Read to the class:

President Woodrow Wilson wanted peace but got war. When he won the presidential election of 1912 and took office on March 4, 1913, he had great plans for reforming the U.S. government and he was not thinking much about other countries. Before becoming president of the United States he had been a professor of political science (government), president of Princeton University, and then governor of New Jersey. Woodrow Wilson was a scholarly individual who liked to study government and come up with solutions to problems. One of the most important bills he signed into law early in his administration was the Federal Reserve Act. This set up the system under which U.S. banks operate, with the Federal Reserve Board raising and lowering interest rates.

President Wilson soon had to turn his attention to Mexico, where revolutions were taking place and various individuals were trying to take control of the government. Pancho Villa led a group of armed men across the border and shot up the town of Columbus, New Mexico, killing American citizens. President Wilson sent the United States Army into Mexico where they tried to catch Pancho Villa but never did.

A more serious situation occurred in Europe when World War I broke out. President Wilson tried to keep the U.S. out of the conflict and was elected to a second term using the slogan, "He kept us out of war." With German submarines sinking American ships, President Wilson on April 2, 1917, made a speech to Congress asking Congress to declare war on Germany. On April 6, 1917, Congress voted to go to war. The U.S. entered World War I on the side of the Allies, which were England, France, and other countries, against Germany and other countries.

When the Allies won the war, President Wilson went to France to personally help negotiate the terms of peace. One of the things he wanted was an organization of countries that would join together and prevent future wars. President Wilson got his *League of Nations* but he could not get the United States Senate to approve the United States joining it. While campaigning across the United States to try to get Americans to encourage the Senate to join the League, President Wilson suffered a stroke. He was never the same again, and it is thought that his wife and some of his advisers helped him make his decisions until he finished his time in office.

Later, after World War II ended in 1945, the United States took the lead in establishing the United Nations, which is similar to the League of Nations that President Wilson had proposed many years earlier.

2. Have students copy the following:

Woodrow Wilson (1856–1924)

Twenty-eighth president (1913–1921)

When German submarines torpedoed American ships, President Wilson asked Congress to declare war on Germany.

Our side won World War I, and President Wilson went to France to help write the peace treaty.

President Wilson got the winning countries to set up a League of Nations.

The U.S. Senate would not approve the United States joining the League of Nations.

3. Have the students copy the following and give them 5 to 10 minutes to write an answer:

How important is the president's spouse and how much influence should the spouse have? Explain your answer.

4. Have students read and discuss their answers or draw a picture about Woodrow Wilson or do both.

Exercise 17: "America" ("My Country 'Tis of Thee")

1. Say to the class:

"Some songs have become a part of our heritage, passed from one generation to the next. The song 'America,' which is commonly called by the song's first line, 'My Country 'Tis of Thee,' has been a part of our heritage since July 4, 1831, when it was first sung in public at the Park Street Church in Boston. The words were written by Samuel Francis Smith, who became a Baptist minister. The melody was taken from and is the same as the British national anthem, 'God Save the King.' I am going to read you the first and last stanzas of the song, and I want you to listen carefully."

2. Read to the class:

My country 'tis of thee,
Sweet land of liberty,
Of thee I sing.
Land where my fathers died,
Land of the Pilgrims' pride,
From ev'ry mountain side,
Let freedom ring!

Our fathers' God, to Thee,
Author of liberty,
To thee we sing.
Long may our land be bright
With freedom's holy light;
Protect us by Thy might,
Great God, our King!

3. Say to the class: "I am going to read you those 2 stanzas again and I want you to choose 1 line or 2 lines to write on your paper. Then I want you to write what you think the part of the song you have chosen means."

4. Read the stanzas to the class again.

5. After giving students 5 to 10 minutes to do their writing, have them read their papers to the class and discuss or have each student draw a picture about the song or do both.

Exercise 18: "America the Beautiful"

1. Say to the class:

"Some songs have become a part of our heritage, passed from one generation to the next. The words to the song 'America the Beautiful' were written by college professor Katherine Lee Bates in 1893 when she and a group of teachers rode mules to the top of Pikes Peak in Colorado. The view from the top of the mountain inspired her to write the words that were later set to music by Samuel A. Ward. I am going to read to you the first and last stanzas of the song and I want you to listen carefully."

2. Read to the class:

O beautiful for spacious skies,
For amber waves of grain,
For purple mountain majesties
Above the fruited plain.
America! America! God shed his grace on thee,
And crown thy good with brotherhood
From sea to shining sea.

O beautiful for patriot dream,
That sees beyond the years,
Thine alabaster cities gleam,
Undimmed by human tears.
America! America! God shed his grace on thee,
And crown thy good with brotherhood
From sea to shining sea.

3. Say to the class:

"I am going to read those 2 stanzas again and I want you to choose 1 line or 2 lines to write on your paper. Then I want you to write what you think the part of the song you have chosen means."

 4. Read the stanzas to the class again.

5. After giving students 5 to 10 minutes to do their writing, have them read their papers to the class and discuss, or have each student draw a picture about the song or do both.

Exercise 19: Army Song and Air Force Song

1. Say to the class:

   "Each of the military services has a special song with which it identifies. These songs are often played when military personnel are involved in a ceremony or parade. Listen carefully while I read some of the words of the Army song and the Air Force song. The Army song tells about caissons. A *caisson* is a two-wheeled, horse-drawn wagon. The Army used to use caissons to carry ammunition and transport artillery. Trucks and other military vehicles replaced caissons. You will still see a caisson used to transport the body of a president or important person as a part of a funeral."

2. Read to the class:

The Army Song

Over hill, over dale
As we hit the dusty trail,
And those caissons go rolling along.
In and out, hear them shout,
"Counter march and right about!"

And the caissons go rolling along.
Then it's hi! hi! hee!
In the field artillery,
Shout out your numbers loud and strong,
For where'er you go,
You will always know
That those caissons go rolling along.

The Air Force Song

Off we go, into the wild blue yonder,
Climbing high, into the sun.
Here they come, zooming to meet our thunder,
At 'em boys, give 'er the gun!
Down we dive, spouting flame from under,
Off with 1 heck of a roar!
We live in fame or go down in flame.
Hey! Nothing can stop the U.S. Air Force!

3. Say to the class:

    "I am going to read again the words that I just read. I want each of you to choose one of the songs and write on your paper what is happening in the song."

 4. Read the songs to the class again.

5. After giving students 5 to 10 minutes to do their writing, have them read their papers to the class and discuss or have each student draw a picture about one or both of the songs or do both.

Exercise 20: Navy Song, Marine Song, Coast Guard Song

1. Say to the class:

    "Each of the military services has a special song with which it identifies. These songs are often played when military personnel are involved in a ceremony or a parade. Listen carefully while I read some of the words to the Navy Song, the Marine Song, and the Coast Guard Song. The motto of the Marines is *Semper Fidelis*, which is Latin for 'always faithful.' The Coast Guard motto is *Semper Paratus*, Latin for 'always ready.' To 'weigh anchor' means to pull up the anchor that holds a ship in place so the ship can sail away. 'Halls of Montezuma' refers to Marines fighting in Mexico during the Mexican War of 1846 to 1848. 'Shores of Tripoli' refers to Marines fighting the Barbary pirates on the coast of the country of Tripoli in the early 1800s."

 2. Read to the class:

The Navy Song

Anchors aweigh, my boys, anchors away.
Farewell to college joys, we sail at break of day-ay-ay-ay.
Through our last night on shore, drink to the foam.
Until we meet once more,
Here's wishing you a happy voyage home.

The Marine Song

From the Halls of Montezuma to the shores of Tripoli
We fight our country's battles in the air, on land, and sea.
First to fight for right and freedom, and to keep our honor clean
We are proud to claim the title of United States Marines.

The Coast Guard Song

We're always ready for the call,
We place our trust in Thee.
Through howling gale, shot, and shell,
To win our victory.
'Semper Paratus' is our guide,
Our pledge, our motto, too.
We're 'Always Ready,' do or die!
Aye! Coast Guard, we fight for you.

3. Say to the class:

   "I am going to read again the words that I just read. I want each of you to choose one of the songs and write on your paper what is happening in the song."

4. Read the songs to the class again.

5. After giving students 5 to 10 minutes to do their writing, have them read their papers to the class and discuss or have each student draw a picture about one or more of the songs or do both.

Exercise 21: Warren Harding

1. Read to the class:

Warren Harding was one of the most popular presidents in the history of the United States, but after he died unexpectedly a little over 2 years into his term of office, his reputation plunged so far that he is thought by some historians to be one of the worst presidents. How did handsome, likable, everybody's friend Warren Harding sink to the bottom of presidential reputations?

Warren Harding, owner and publisher of a small-town newspaper, was easy to get along with and tried to never offend anyone. After getting elected to local offices, he eventually became a U.S. senator from Ohio. When the Republicans had their convention in 1920 to choose a presidential candidate, they had trouble agreeing on who should get the nomination. Neither of the 2 leading contenders could get enough votes to win the nomination and neither would drop out. Finally, at a meeting of party leaders in a hotel room, they decided that the deadlock would be broken by giving the nomination to Warren Harding. Who could object to the nomination of a man who was so popular? Harding was elected president by a landslide. He campaigned on the slogan of returning the country to "normalcy." Americans had just been through World War I, and they liked the idea of a friendly, likable president who would let Americans enjoy being Americans and leave the rest of the world alone. President Harding's popularity continued for the 2 years he was president, but about the time he died it was starting to be known that some of the men that he had appointed to high positions in the government were making shady deals and stealing from the government. President Harding may have not known what they were doing until shortly before his death.

In the summer of 1923 the president and his wife took a trip to the West Coast and then traveled by boat to Alaska. On the way back from Alaska the president got violently ill and was taken to a hotel in San Francisco. Some think it was food poisoning. Some think it was a heart attack. Some even believe that his wife or somebody else might have poisoned him. Whatever the cause, President Harding died in San Francisco on August 2, 1923, and a nation that did not yet fully know about the dishonest things that had gone on in his administration mourned him greatly.

2. Have students copy the following:

Warren Harding (1865–1923)

Twenty-ninth president (1921–1923)

He was a very popular president when he was alive.

Some of the friends he appointed to high office were dishonest and did illegal things.

President Harding died in San Francisco after becoming seriously ill on his way back from a trip to Alaska.

After his death President Harding's reputation dropped because of the dishonest things that had gone on during his administration.

3. Have students copy the following and give them 5 or 10 minutes to write an answer:

Should a person be held responsible for what his or her friends do? Why or why not?

4. Have students read and discuss their answers or draw a picture about Warren Harding or do both.

Exercise 22: Calvin Coolidge

1. Read to the class:

When President Warren Harding died unexpectedly in 1923, Vice President Calvin Coolidge was visiting his father, a justice of the peace in Plymouth, Vermont. On receiving the news of Harding's death, Calvin was awakened by his father at about 2:30 A.M. After Coolidge had dressed and knelt in prayer, his father, acting in his capacity as a justice of the peace and notary public, swore him in as president of the United States. President Harding had been outgoing and friendly, enjoyed playing golf and poker, and liked a good joke and laugh. President Coolidge was quiet by nature, didn't believe in frivolous pursuits, and believed in not wasting money or anything else. The story is told in several forms, the most common being that a woman dinner guest at the White House said, "I've made a bet that I can get you to say more than 3 words." President Coolidge replied, "You lose." There is also the story of a woman who, when told that former President Calvin Coolidge had died, asked, "How could they tell?" President Coolidge had the nickname "Silent Cal," and it suited him well. Nevertheless, he made speeches on the radio, allowed photographers to take his picture, and held press conferences because he thought it was his duty as president to do so. In spite of his quiet nature and dislike of being the center of attention, he was a very popular president. He thought that the best thing a president could do was to get the government out of people's lives and let people get on with the business of making a living. He once said, "The chief business of the American people is business." He believed in low taxes and low government spending. He believed that people should be responsible for themselves and that average Americans would do well and be happy if there were large businesses to employ them. In 1928, having served out the remainder of Warren Harding's term and then serving a term of his own, Silent Cal announced, "I do not choose to run." Big businesses had boomed and the country had prospered during his time in office, so it is very likely he could have been elected again without campaigning much or saying much.

2. Have students copy the following:

   Calvin Coolidge (1871–1933)

   Thirtieth president (1923–1929)

   He was quiet and frugal by nature.

   He thought the government should not waste money and should stay out of people's lives as much as possible.

   He thought that big businesses were good for America and Americans.

   Americans and the economy prospered during the time Calvin Coolidge was president.

3. Have students copy the following and give them 5 to 10 minutes to write an answer:

   What things should the government do for people and what things should people do for themselves?

4. Have students read and discuss their answers or draw a picture about Calvin Coolidge or do both.

Exercise 23: Herbert Hoover

1. Read to the class:

When Herbert Hoover was sworn in as president on March 4, 1929, the United States was in a period of great prosperity. Americans were making money and they expected to go on making money. Unforeseen was a great danger to the nation's businesses and jobs, like a shark waiting to devour the economy that had been sailing briskly along. That shark was the stock market. People had been buying shares of stock on credit. If, for example, you wanted to buy a share of stock in a company that manufactured bicycles and the share of stock cost $1, you might only have to put up a dime; the other 90 cents would be loaned to you by the stock-broker. That was great, so long as the company was making money selling lots of bicycles and giving you your share of profits so that you could pay off the 90 cents you had borrowed. Of course, if the company was making lots of money, the price of a share of stock would go up and you could sell your share of stock, getting back the original dime you had invested and maybe make an additional nickel or dime from the sale. It seemed so easy to make money by buying and selling shares of stock that all kinds of people wanted to do it. But then businesses started slowing down because they weren't able to sell all that they were producing. Investors in the stock market started selling off their shares of stock because the price of stocks was starting to go down and they wanted to sell before the price dropped even further. Panic among investors in the stock market set in, with practically everybody wanting to sell shares. The price of stocks plummeted. Yesterday, many people had been rich because of what they owned in the stock market. Now they were penniless. Some of the formerly rich people, now paupers, committed suicide. The stock market crashed on October 29, 1929, less than 8 months after Herbert Hoover had been sworn in as president. When businesses closed and people lost their jobs they blamed the president. This period, known as the *Great Depression,* lasted throughout the 1930s. Over 25 percent of workers were unemployed, and those who had jobs usually did not make a lot of money. People lost homes, men and boys roamed the country in search of work, and life was very hard for many Americans. President Hoover thought that private charities and local governments, like cities and counties, could provide the help people needed. President Hoover thought that the economy would get better and people would get back to work, but things didn't get better. President Hoover became very unpopular and was defeated in 1932 when he ran for reelection.

2. Have students copy the following:

Herbert Hoover (1874–1964)

Thirty-first president (1929–1933)

The stock market crashed in 1929 and the Great Depression started.

Businesses closed, people lost jobs, and times were very hard for most Americans.

President Hoover thought that private charities and local governments could give people the help they needed.

Many people blamed President Hoover for the Depression and he was defeated when he ran for reelection in 1932.

3. Have students copy the following and give them 5 to 10 minutes to write an answer:

Should a president be blamed for an economic depression? Why or why not?

4. Have students read and discuss their answers or draw a picture about Herbert Hoover or do both.

Exercise 24: Franklin D. Roosevelt

Copyright © 2006 by John Wiley & Sons, Inc.

Read Aloud

1. Read to the class:

All presidents face difficult challenges. None, with perhaps the exception of Abraham Lincoln, who was president when the country was divided in Civil War, faced more difficult challenges than Franklin Roosevelt. Even President James Madison, who was forced to flee Washington, D.C., when the British captured the city in 1814 and burned what was later rebuilt and renamed the White House, had to endure the War of 1812 for only 2 years of his 8 years in office. During Franklin Roosevelt's 12 years in office the United States was in constant danger. During the 1930s the United States was in danger of total economic collapse as people suffered the Great Depression. Then, the United States entered World War II as the Depression ended. If the U.S. and its allies lost World War II, Nazi Germany and its chief ally Japan would control the world.

Franklin Roosevelt, or *FDR* as he was often called by his initials, was accustomed to challenges. Stricken with polio at the age of 39 and never able to walk again, FDR forced himself to reenter public life and served as governor of New York before winning the presidential election of 1932. With the country locked in the Great Depression, FDR got Congress to pass a bunch of new laws, some of which worked and some of which didn't work in trying to help out-of-work Americans get back on their feet. One of the laws set up the Social Security system, which is something that nearly every American is familiar with today. Other laws tried to help people keep their homes and provide jobs by building things like huge dams. The Great Depression did not end until the United States started gearing up to fight World War II. After the Japanese bombed Pearl Harbor on December 7, 1941, the United States suffered a series of defeats for about the first 6 months of the war and things looked pretty bad for our side. Then the U.S. started pushing Japanese forces back across the Pacific and helping England and our allies win battles in North Africa and Europe. FDR did not live to see the end of the war. Shortly after being elected to a fourth term of office, with no other president ever serving that long, an exhausted and worn-out FDR suffered what is generally called today a stroke and died on April 12, 1945.

Write on Board

2. Have students copy the following:

Franklin D. Roosevelt (1882–1945)

Thirty-second president (1933–1945)

He was crippled by polio but the disease did not stop him from becoming president and serving longer than any other president.

He was president during the difficult times of the Great Depression and World War II.

He died shortly before World War II ended with the surrender of Germany and Japan.

3. Have students copy the following and give them 5 to 10 minutes to write an answer:

The Twenty-Second Amendment, added to the United States Constitution in 1951, limits a president to being elected president twice. Was this amendment a good idea? Why or why not?

4. Have students read and discuss their answers or draw a picture about Franklin Roosevelt or do both.

Chapter Seven

Fifth Grade Lesson Plans

Exercise 1: The Heart

Read Aloud

1. Read to the class:

Your body is alive. You say, "Of course my body is alive. I'm alive. I can wiggle my finger. I can turn my head and see things in different locations." But there is more to your body's being alive than just the things that can be observed on the outside of the body. All kinds of things are going on inside your body, and you are not even aware of many of them. To mention only a few: Your immune system is fighting off invaders that are trying to make you sick. Oxygen is being carried to all parts of your body. Food is broken into molecules and going into your bloodstream to provide you with energy.

The power plant inside your body that keeps all of the many internal functions of your body in operation is your heart. When your heart is no longer able to beat, you die, internally and externally. Your heart beats about 100,000 times each day. Just think how many heartbeats you will have during your lifetime. When we say your heart is beating, we mean it is contracting and then expanding. Your heart is like a couple of pumps that operate side by side. Each pump consists of 2 parts: the upper part is called the *atrium* and the larger lower part is called the *ventricle*. Blood in the right atrium is sent into the right ventricle, where it is then sent to the lungs to pick up oxygen. The oxygenated blood then goes to the left atrium, and then to the left ventricle, where it is pumped through the aorta at the top of the heart and sent throughout the body to deliver oxygen and nutrients. The deoxygenated blood then returns to the right atrium to go through the whole circulatory process again. Wow! Sounds like a lot of blood moving about. No, there are only about 10 to 12 pints in the average adult male, 8 to 9 pints in the average adult female, and less in children.

2. Have students copy the following:

The Heart

The heart is the organ that circulates blood throughout the body.

The right side of the heart pumps blood to the lungs to pick up oxygen.

The left side of the heart pumps the oxygenated blood throughout the body.

The deoxygenated blood returns to the right side of the heart to start the process all over.

Your heart beats about 100,000 times each day.

The average adult male has 10 to 12 pints of blood, the average adult female has 8 to 9 pints, and children have less.

3. Have students copy the following and give them 5 to 10 minutes to make their lists:

List 10 things that you need a healthy heart to do.

4. Have students read their lists to the class and discuss or have each student draw a picture about 1 or more of the things he or she has listed or have them do both.

Exercise 2: The Lungs

1. Read to the class:

We live in a sea of air. The sea of air extends about 600 miles up from the surface of the Earth, but it is only the bottom layer, the troposphere, where living things can breathe normally. Above the troposphere, which extends up 12 miles at the equator, humans must take measures to ensure that they have oxygen or they will die. Have you ever been swimming and committed the unwise and dangerous act of staying underwater too long? Until you kicked yourself upward and broke through the surface, your lungs felt like they were bursting. When your head was again in the air, you gulped air as fast as you could to relieve the discomfort that had been growing in your body along with the danger signals that if you didn't get oxygen soon, you would become unconscious and die.

Our lungs take in air and combine oxygen with blood so that the heart can send the oxygenated blood throughout the body. Your body has 2 lungs. The right lung has 3 lobes (parts) and the left only 2. In each of these lungs are a lot of little air passages and little blood vessels that lead to tiny spaces called *alveoli*. When air gets to an alveolus it is combined with blood, then the oxygenated blood goes to the heart. The heart pumps blood throughout the body to deliver oxygen and nutrients that cells in your body need to stay alive.

The lungs of a baby at birth are pinkish-white. The lungs turn darker as air is breathed in throughout life. Some people pollute their lungs by smoking, which can lead to terrible diseases like emphysema and lung cancer. Before the 1950s people were largely unaware of the dangers of smoking, but now there is no reason for people not to know that smoking damages the air passages, blood vessels, and tiny alveoli. People should not abuse their lungs if they want to live long and healthy lives.

2. Have students copy the following:

    The Lungs

    Lungs breathe in air, combine oxygen with blood, and breathe out carbon dioxide.

    The right lung has 3 lobes and the left only 2.

    Each lung has a lot of little air passages, little blood vessels, and little spaces called alveoli.

    Each alveolus combines oxygen with blood so that the oxygenated blood can go to the heart and be shipped out to the cells in the body.

    Smoking damages the lungs and can lead to serious illnesses.

3. Have students copy the following and give them 5 to 10 minutes to make their lists:

    List 10 reasons why smoking is something you should not do.

4. Have students read their lists to the class and discuss or have each student draw a picture about 1 or more of the things he or she has listed or have them do both.

Exercise 3: The Liver

1. Read to the class:

When food drops into your stomach, enzymes and gastric juices help speed up the breaking down of the food as the stomach churns the food into a fluid called *chyme*. When the chyme leaves the stomach and goes into the small intestine, the gallbladder sends bile into the mixture, and the pancreas adds enzymes and other things to further process the food. The bile that the gallbladder sent into the small intestine came from the liver. The body can function without the gallbladder, and in fact many people have operations to remove their gallbladder when it is not functioning properly. The liver is not optional; you must have a functioning liver to survive.

The liver is your largest internal organ and is located in the upper part of your abdomen. The liver is unique among internal organs in that it can regenerate in the case of injury or illness. That means it can grow new tissue to replace damaged tissue. Although it can renew about 80 percent of its total size, liver diseases, such as cirrhosis, which is often caused by excessive drinking of alcohol for a number of years, can make the liver unable to function and unable to regenerate. Some people are lucky enough to get a liver transplant. Those who cannot usually die.

In addition to producing bile, the liver processes glucose, proteins, vitamins, fats, and most of the compounds that are carried by the blood throughout the body. It stores glucose, a sugar substance that in stored form is called *glycogen* and dispenses it when you need energy. The liver purifies blood and usually has about a pint of blood being processed in it at any given time. The liver removes poisonous and harmful substances from the blood, absorbing them into bile that can be carried out of the body. Obviously, the liver cannot remove all poisons or drugs that enter the body and some people die from being poisoned. This does not detail all of the important things the liver does, but perhaps you now have an idea of how the liver functions to keep you active and healthy.

2. Have students copy the following:

The Liver

The liver does many important things to keep your body functioning properly.

It processes and stores glucose in the form of glycogen, and dispenses it when you need energy.

It processes proteins, vitamins, fats, and most of the compounds that are carried by the blood throughout the body.

It purifies blood.

It dispenses bile to aid in digestion and discard poisonous substances.

The liver is the only internal organ that can regenerate itself.

A functioning liver is necessary to keep you alive.

3. Have the students copy the following and give them 5 to 10 minutes to compose their poems:

Make up a short poem about your liver.

4. Have students read and discuss their poems or have each student draw a picture about his or her poem or have them do both.

Exercise 4: The Kidneys

Read Aloud)))

1. Read to the class:

A person has 2 kidneys, which is fortunate because if 1 fails the other can take over the entire workload. Some people even donate kidneys to other people so that individuals who have lost the use of both kidneys can continue to live. What do kidneys do that you need at least 1 functioning kidney to stay alive? The kidneys, located toward the back, one on the right side of the abdomen and the other on the left, are fist-sized organs that filter waste and fluid from the blood. The kidneys are somewhat like a water treatment plant, removing from the blood waste products and things that are bad for the body. The kidneys allow a certain amount of water and things that are good for the body to pass on in the blood. The waste product is called urine. Each kidney has a tube called a "ureter" through which the urine passes to the bladder. The bladder stores the urine until it is sent out through the urethra when a person urinates.

People with severe kidney disorders may undergo dialysis. In *hemodialysis* a person is hooked up to a machine and the blood from the person's body passes through the machine where it is purified before being passed back into the body.

In *peritoneal dialysis* a small hollow tube is inserted into an incision that has been made in the abdomen. The tube remains in place and a special dialysis fluid is poured into the abdomen through the tube. The fluid is left in place for a while and then drained. Hemodialysis usually takes place at a medical facility, lasts about 3 or 4 hours, and is done about 3 times a week. Peritoneal dialysis can be done at home, takes about an hour, and is commonly done about 4 times a day.

2. Have students copy the following:

   The Kidneys

   A person has 2 kidneys and can survive with only 1 if 1 of the 2 fails.

   Blood is purified by passing through the kidneys.

   The kidneys regulate the amount of water they allow to continue on in the blood along with the things they don't remove that are good for the body.

   Waste products in the form of urine are sent through the ureter from the kidney to the bladder.

   The urine leaves the bladder through the urethra when a person urinates.

   People with severe kidney problems may undergo dialysis.

3. Have students copy the following and give them 5 to 10 minutes to write an answer:

   What things should a person consider if that person is thinking about whether or not to donate a kidney to another person?

4. Have students read and discuss their answers or have each student draw a picture about kidneys or do both.

Exercise 5: Harry Truman

1. Read to the class:

Vice President Harry Truman unexpectedly became president on April 12, 1945, when President Franklin D. Roosevelt died less than 3 months after being inaugurated for his fourth term of office. Harry Truman was taking over at a time when World War II had not yet been won. A little less than a month later Germany surrendered on May 7, 1945, which became known as *V-E Day,* meaning victory in Europe. The Japanese and Americans were still locked in a bloody battle in the Pacific. By the end of June 1945, after a battle that had lasted about 3 months, Americans managed to defeat the Japanese on the island of Okinawa. In the battle for Okinawa over 7,000 American soldiers and Marines were killed and over 31,000 wounded. This did not include the more than 4,000 U.S. sailors killed and 7,000 U.S. sailors wounded on ships in the waters around Okinawa. It is estimated that about 110,000 Japanese died in the battle for Okinawa.

President Truman was told that the United States had developed the atomic bomb, a new powerful weapon that was more destructive than any weapon the world had ever known. President Truman hoped to end the war by using the atomic bomb if Japan refused to surrender. He knew that dropping the atomic bomb on Japan would kill thousands, maybe even hundreds of thousands of Japanese, but it would also save hundreds of thousands, maybe even over a million lives of Americans and Japanese if United States soldiers and Marines did not have to fight the Japanese any further to defeat Japan. He warned the Japanese to surrender or be destroyed. The Japanese ignored President Truman's warning and United States bombers dropped 2 atomic bombs on Japan. The first bomb was dropped on the city of Hiroshima. Three days later when the Japanese had not surrendered, a second bomb was dropped on the city of Nagasaki. Although the exact number of people killed by the 2 bombs is unknown, it is estimated that somewhere between 100,000 and 200,000 people were killed. After the second bomb was dropped, the Japanese surrendered, ending World War II.

In Europe, what was called the *cold war* started. The Soviet Union (most of which is now Russia) would not get out of the countries of Eastern Europe it had taken over while fighting as our ally against the Germans in World War II. The United States and England quickly gave France, Belgium, and other countries of Western Europe their independence as Allied armies liberated them from the Germans. For over 40 years after World War II the United States and the countries of Western Europe faced the Soviets (Russians) across what became known as the *Iron Curtain*. The Iron Curtain was an armed border set up by the Soviets to separate Soviet-controlled Eastern Europe from the free countries of Western Europe.

The United States gave billions of dollars in aid to feed, rebuild, and strengthen Western Europe after World War II. The aid program was called the *Marshall Plan,* named after the U.S. secretary of state at that time. In 1948 and 1949 the United States and England flew planeload after planeload of food and supplies to West Berlin to keep the Soviets from starving the West Berliners into submission to the Soviets. American airmen often dropped chewing gum and candy to the children there, who eagerly watched the planes fly overhead.

On the other side of the world the United States went to war to defend noncommunist South Korea, which had been invaded by communist North Korea. President Truman, who had ordered the dropping of the atomic bombs on Japan to end World War II, refused to use the atomic bomb in the Korean conflict, fearing that it might lead to World War III with the Soviet Union and communist China, both of which supported North Korea. The war had been raging for over 2 years when President Truman, who had served nearly 8 years in office, decided not to run for reelection. The war in Korea was a war he did not want to lose, but couldn't seem to win.

Dwight Eisenhower won the election against Adlai Stevenson and became president on January 20, 1953. Six months later, communist North Korea agreed to a cease-fire. The death of Soviet dictator Joseph Stalin may have influenced North Korea's decision to stop fighting. Many people believe that President Eisenhower had threatened to use the atomic bomb if North Korea did not agree to a truce.

2. Have students copy the following:

   Harry Truman (1884–1972)

   Thirty-third president (1945–1953)

   He made the decision to drop the atomic bomb on Japan in World War II.

The U.S. in its Marshall Plan gave billions of dollars in aid to feed, strengthen, and rebuild Western Europe after World War II.

The U.S. and England in 1948 and 1949 flew food and supplies into West Berlin to keep the Soviets (Russians) from starving the people of West Berlin into submission.

In 1950 President Truman sent American troops to defend South Korea after South Korea had been attacked by communist North Korea.

3. Have students copy the following and give them 5 to 10 minutes to write an answer:

Was President Truman's decision to drop the atomic bomb on Japan a good decision? Why or why not?

4. Have students read their answers to the class and discuss or have each student draw a picture about Harry Truman or have them do both.

Exercise 6: Dwight Eisenhower

1. Read to the class:

When Dwight Eisenhower ran for president in 1952, he said that if he were elected he would go to Korea. This was a very popular thing to say to voters, because the United States had been involved in a war in Korea for more than 2 years. Dwight Eisenhower had been the general in charge of the D-Day landings during World War II. D-Day was on June 6, 1944. On that day, over 4,000 ships carried more than 150,000 soldiers across the English Channel to attack the German soldiers who had conquered France. General Eisenhower had commanded the millions of soldiers it had taken to defeat Hitler's Nazi Germany. If anyone could end the war in Korea, American voters thought, it was General Eisenhower, popularly known as "Ike." General Eisenhower ran on the campaign slogan "I like Ike" and was overwhelmingly elected. He did go to Korea, and several months later communist North Korea agreed to a truce, which made President Eisenhower even more popular.

It was good to have a former general as president for 8 years, because the United States and the Soviet Union were engaged in the *cold war.* During the cold war, the two nations didn't fight each other in an all-out war of armies; instead, each side built up military weapons, trying to keep the other side from having a military advantage. The Soviet Union had an economic system called *communism,* in which the government owned all the businesses and had strict control over people's lives. The United States did not like communist countries, and communist countries did not like the United States. The United States worried that communist countries would take over other countries and maybe even try to take over the United States. The U.S. developed a policy called *containment,* which meant that it wanted to keep the communist countries from expanding beyond their own borders. From the end of World War II in 1945 until the end of the 1980s, it looked as if the United States and the Soviet Union might go to war at any time. Then, in 1991, the Soviet Union gave up communism and some parts of it broke up into countries that were independent. The Soviet Union changed its name back to Russia, which is what it was called before the communists took over in 1917. The United States and Russia became friendlier and cut back on military weapons.

Although the United States in the 1950s did not get along well with the Soviet Union and other communist countries, President Eisenhower got many friendly countries to cooperate on defense and other matters. Cooperation between the U.S. and Canada led to the building of the St. Lawrence Seaway, which made it possible to travel the St. Lawrence River between Canada and the United States. President Eisenhower also made traveling across the United States easier by getting Congress to pass a bill, which he signed into law, authorizing the building of highways across the United States. You may be familiar with I-70, I-80, I-10, or some other part of the interstate (I) highways we have today.

In the 1950s, some parts of the United States had separate schools for black children. In 1954 the United States Supreme Court decided that having separate schools was wrong. They made this decision in a case commonly called *Brown v. the Board of Education.* Some schools ignored this ruling. In 1957, Little Rock High School, an all-white school in Arkansas, would not let blacks enter to start the fall term. President Eisenhower sent U.S. Army troops to escort the black students into the school. During the 1950s and 1960s Martin Luther King Jr., a black Baptist minister, led demonstrations to end racial segregation in the southern part of the country.

While President Eisenhower was in office during the 1950s, Elvis Presley and other entertainers performed a new kind of music: rock 'n' roll. As we have seen, a lot of important things were going on besides "the birth of rock 'n' roll."

2. Have students copy the following:

   Dwight Eisenhower (1890–1969)

   Thirty-fourth president (1953–1961)

   He had been the general in charge of the D-Day landings on June 6, 1944, during World War II.

   North Korea agreed to a truce to stop fighting in Korea several months after he became president.

   He signed laws that authorized the building of the St. Lawrence Seaway and the interstate highway system.

   He sent U.S. Army troops to Little Rock High School in 1957 to force the school to admit black students.

3. Have students copy the following and give them 5 to 10 minutes to write an answer:

   What do you think was the most important thing Dwight Eisenhower accomplished during his life? Explain why you think it is the most important.

4. Have students read their answers to the class and discuss or have each student draw a picture about Dwight Eisenhower or have them do both.

Exercise 7: John Kennedy

Read Aloud))

1. Read to the class:

When John Kennedy was president, the United States and the Soviet Union almost went to war. It is very fortunate that they did not, because it is possible that a war between the 2 most powerful nations in the world could have destroyed everybody. The island of Cuba, approximately 90 miles from the coast of Florida, was the place that caused the near-collision of the 2 superpowers. Cuba had become a communist country after a man named Fidel Castro had led a successful revolution and overthrown the former government in 1959. Because the government that Fidel Castro set up was communist and the Soviet Union was communist, the countries were friends and cooperated with each other. The Soviet Union in 1962 decided to place nuclear missiles in Cuba and point them at the United States. When the United States found out that the Soviets were building missile launching pads in Cuba, President Kennedy told the Soviet leader, Nikita Khrushchev, that the United States would not let Soviet ships bring in the things necessary to complete the missile sites. Nikita Khrushchev ignored President Kennedy's warning, and Soviet ships kept sailing toward Cuba. President Kennedy ordered the U.S. Navy not to let the Soviet ships pass. The Soviet ships sailed on toward the U.S. blockade and the world waited to see if the world was going to explode in nuclear war. After several tense days the Soviet ships turned back and people rejoiced that World War III had not started.

Another area of competition between Americans and Soviets was space exploration. On May 25, 1961, President Kennedy said in a speech that the United States would land a man on the moon by the end of the decade. The United States achieved the goal when astronaut Neil Armstrong stepped on the surface of the moon on July 20, 1969, and said, "That's one small step for man, one giant leap for mankind."

Theodore Roosevelt had been the youngest president ever when, as vice president at the age of 42, he took over for the assassinated President William McKinley. John Kennedy was the youngest person ever elected to the office of president, winning the election at age 43. John Kennedy became president at a very young age for presidents and he also died at what is considered a young age. On November 22, 1963, President Kennedy and his wife Jacqueline were riding in the back seat of a convertible in Dallas, Texas, where they were visiting. Somebody shot the president with a rifle. Later, it was ruled that a man named Lee Harvey Oswald had done the shooting. Jack Ruby, a nightclub owner, while standing in a crowd of onlookers while Oswald was being walked from 1 place to another in police custody, lunged forward from the crowd and fired a pistol, killing Oswald. Jack Ruby, months later while in jail, became ill and died. Many people still think there are unanswered questions surrounding the death of President Kennedy.

Although John Kennedy died at the age of 46, he accomplished many things during his shortened life. He had been a war hero in World War II as a commander of a PT boat. He had won a Pulitzer Prize in literature for writing the book *Profiles in Courage*. He had served 6 years in the U.S. House of Representatives and 8 years in the U.S. Senate. He was the first Roman Catholic ever elected president of the United States.

2. Have students copy the following:

   John Kennedy (1917–1963)

   Thirty-fifth president (1961–1963)

   He pledged the United States to the goal of landing a man on the moon by the end of the 1960s.

   He stopped the Soviet Union from putting nuclear missiles in Cuba.

   He was assassinated in Dallas, Texas, on November 22, 1963.

   He was the first Roman Catholic elected president.

3. Have students copy the following and give them 5 to 10 minutes to write an answer:

   Should the religion of a person running for president be of any concern to voters? Why or why not?

4. Have students read their answers to the class and discuss or have each student draw a picture about John Kennedy or have them do both.

Exercise 8: Lyndon Johnson

Read Aloud)))   1. Read to the class:

Vice President Lyndon Johnson was sworn in as president aboard Air Force One, the presidential airplane that was taking the casket and body of President Kennedy from Dallas back to Washington, D.C., along with his widow Jacqueline Kennedy. President Kennedy had just been assassinated, and the nation was in shock. President Johnson, through words and actions, tried to reassure the country by carrying on the job of president in much the same way he thought President Kennedy would have. He kept President Kennedy's cabinet members instead of appointing new ones, and he tried to get Congress to pass the bills that President Kennedy had wanted passed.

In the presidential election of 1964, President Johnson won overwhelmingly, getting over 60 percent of the popular vote and defeating his opponent, Barry Goldwater, by 486 electoral votes to 52 electoral votes. President Lyndon Johnson felt firmly in control and pursued a program that became known as the Great Society. Lyndon Johnson's family had not been rich when he was growing up, and as a young man he had lived through the Great Depression when many Americans were out of work and poor. President Johnson wanted to eliminate poverty so he declared what he called "a war on poverty." He got Congress to pass bills that he signed into law to spend money on welfare, cities, education, health care, and many other things to try to end poverty. He also got Congress to pass civil rights legislation, laws that helped blacks and other Americans get equal treatment.

While President Johnson was waging a war on poverty, he also waged a war against communist North Vietnam. The country of Vietnam had been split into 2 parts: communist North Vietnam and noncommunist South Vietnam. Communist North Vietnam was intent on reuniting the country and making it all communist. Guerrilla fighters, known as *Vietcong,* started waging war on South Vietnam, blowing up things in cities, attacking small villages or whatever they could, and then fading into the countryside or blending in with the population. Under Presidents Eisenhower and Kennedy, American military personnel had been sent to observe and advise the South Vietnamese on how to defeat the Vietcong and the North Vietnamese regular army.

The war kept getting bigger, and neither side could conquer the other side. Over half a million Americans were fighting in the war. In January 1968, battles started all over South Vietnam in what became known as the *Tet offensive.* A truce had been declared so that the Vietnamese could celebrate the holiday time of the lunar new year. The communists violated the truce and attacked at many places. American and South Vietnamese forces won the battles, but many Americans in the United States, watching the events on television, thought America should get out of the war immediately to stop the bloodshed.

In the United States, in addition to thousands of people marching in the streets to demonstrate against the war, parts of some cities had been erupting in riots of black people burning, looting, and fighting against police officers. It was a very troubled time in America and on March 31, 1968, President Johnson announced on television: "I shall not seek, and will not accept, the nomination of my party for another term as your president."

The Vietnam War would go on for the American troops for another 5 years until the withdrawal of American troops was completed in 1973, the same year Lyndon Johnson died of a heart attack in Texas. In 1975, North Vietnam won a complete victory over South Vietnam and the entire country came under communist control. Many South Vietnamese fled the country, a lot of them eventually becoming American citizens.

2. Have students copy the following:

Lyndon Johnson (1908–1973)

Thirty-sixth president (1963–1969)

He got laws passed to set up programs to try to end poverty.

He sent American troops to Vietnam to help noncommunist South Korea defend itself against communist North Vietnam.

American and South Vietnamese troops defeated the Vietcong and North Vietnamese Army in battles during the Tet offensive of 1968.

Many Americans wanted the war stopped and protested against the war.

President Johnson decided in 1968 not to run for reelection.

3. Have students copy the following and give them 5 to 10 minutes to write an answer:

The Vietnamese are but 1 of many groups that have fled from other countries to come to the United States. Why do so many people want to come to the United States? Should we let them? Explain your answers.

4. Have students read and discuss their answers or have each student draw a picture about Lyndon Johnson or have them do both.

Exercise 9: "Paul Revere's Ride"

Read Aloud)))
1. Read to the class:

In 1775 there was no United States of America. Instead, there were 13 English colonies that would later become the first 13 states in the United States of America. Before those 13 English colonies would become states, a war for independence would be fought between the colonies and the mother country of England. George Washington would become famous as the general who won the war for the colonies and later would become the country's first president.

The war for independence began before George Washington had even taken command of the army. A group of 70 minutemen farmers stood against an estimated 700 to 1,000 British soldiers at a village called Lexington. Eight of the minutemen were killed before the others dragged their dead and 10 wounded away as the British continued their advance. Minutemen reinforcements arrived and took a stand at a bridge at the village of Concord. The minutemen inflicted enough casualties on the British that the British fled back to Boston.

How did the minutemen get their muskets and await the British soldiers who were coming to arrest their leaders and take away their guns and ammunition? Paul Revere and William Dawes sounded the alarm: "The British are coming!" Paul Revere is the more remembered of the 2 because Henry Wadsworth Longfellow wrote a poem many years later that told of "Paul Revere's Ride." It is a long poem, so I am only going to read parts of the poem and tell you what happened in the parts I do not read.

Read Aloud)))
2. Read the following to the class, along with the explanations:

Paul Revere's Ride

Listen, my children, and you shall hear
Of the midnight ride of Paul Revere,
On the eighteenth of April, in Seventy-five;
Hardly a man is now alive
Who remembers that famous day and year.

He said to his friend, "If the British march
By land or sea from the town to-night,
Hang a lantern aloft on the belfry arch
Of the North Church tower as a signal light—
One if by land, and 2, if by sea;
And I on the opposite shore will be,
Ready to ride and spread the alarm
Through every Middlesex village and farm,
For the country-folk to be up to arm.

[Then Paul Revere gets in a rowboat and rows across the river to await the signal of his friend who is in the church tower watching for the British. The friend signals with 1 lantern that the British are coming by land. Paul Revere jumps on his horse and rides into the night. He rides to farms and villages, warning that the British are on the way.]

You know the rest. In books you have read,
How the British Regulars fired and fled—
How the farmers gave them ball for ball,
From behind each fence and farm-yard wall,
Chasing the red-coats down the lane,
Then crossing the fields to emerge again
Under the trees at the turn of the road,
And only pausing to fire and load.

So through the night rode Paul Revere;
And so through the night went his cry of alarm
To every Middlesex village and farm—
A cry of defiance and not of fear,
A voice in the darkness, a knock at the door,
And a word that shall echo forevermore!
For, borne on that night-wind of the past,
Through all our history, to the last,
In the hours of darkness and peril and need,
The people will waken and listen to hear
The hurrying hoof-beats of the steed,
And the midnight message of Paul Revere.

3. Tell the students that you want them to copy and try to memorize the first stanza of the poem as you write the first stanza on the board.

4. After students have completed copying the stanza, erase the stanza and have individual students try to recite it from memory (obviously, without looking at their papers).

5. Have students copy the following and give them 5 to 10 minutes to write an answer:

   Why would 70 minutemen farmers be willing to get their muskets and go out and face a force of at least 10 times as many British soldiers when the farmers knew that they might be killed by the soldiers?

6. Have students read their answers to the class and discuss or have each student draw a picture about "Paul Revere's Ride" or have the students do both.

Exercise 10: "Old Ironsides"

Read Aloud)))   1. Read to the class:

The oldest ship in the United States Navy is the USS *Constitution*. Its service dates back to 1797. Why do we still have a sailing ship on active duty in the United States that is so old and outdated that it could easily be destroyed by any modern warship? A poem saved the USS *Constitution* from destruction and the ship has managed to survive to this day and perhaps will survive as long as there is a United States Navy. When the U.S. fought the British in the War of 1812, the British had the most powerful navy in the world. The USS *Constitution* was, for its time, a modern, well-constructed ship. It won some outstanding victories against British ships and survived the war without being captured or destroyed. The sturdy wood sides of the ship ended the war without serious damage from the cannonballs fired at it from the enemy ships during battles, thus earning it the nickname "Old Ironsides." But Old Ironsides did become old. By 1830 it was 33 years old and the navy was ready to scrap it in favor of newer ships.

Twenty-one-year-old Oliver Wendell Holmes thought the old ship deserved a better fate than being taken out of active service and taken apart to reuse whatever of its parts that could be of use in some way. He wrote a poem expressing his feelings about Old Ironsides. The poem was published in many newspapers and aroused people to protest the ship's planned fate. The decision was reversed, and Old Ironsides remains a part of the United States Navy today. It sails only occasionally from where it is berthed on the East Coast, never again to do battle for the United States. It is maintained and ready to sail, but most of the time it remains dockside, allowing visitors to come aboard and see the U.S. Navy ship that is over 200 years old.

Read Aloud)))   2. Read to the class:

Old Ironsides
Ay, tear her tattered ensign down!
Long has it waved on high,
And many an eye has danced to
That banner in the sky;
Beneath it rung the battle shout,
And burst the cannon's roar—
The meteor of the air
Shall sweep the clouds no more.

Her decks, once red with heroes' blood
Where knelt the vanquished foe,
When winds were hurrying o'er the flood,
And waves were white below,
No more shall feel the victor's tread,
Or know the conquered knee—
The harpies of the shore shall pluck
The eagle of the sea!

Oh, better that her shattered hulk
Should sink beneath the wave;
Her thunders shook the mighty deep,
And there should be her grave;
Nail to the mast her holy flag,
Set every threadbare sail,
And give her to the god of storms,
The lightning and the gale!

 3. Tell the students that you want them to copy and try to memorize the first stanza of the poem as you write the first stanza on the board.

4. After the students have completed copying the stanza, erase the stanza and have students try to recite it from memory (obviously, without looking at their papers).

 5. Have students copy the following and give them 5 to 10 minutes to write an answer:

Is it a waste of money for the United States Navy to keep in service a ship that is over 200 years old? Why or why not?

6. Have the students read their answers to the class and discuss or have each student draw a picture about Old Ironsides or have the students do both.

Exercise 11: "The Ship of State"

 1. Read to the class:

When people write or speak, they sometimes compare one thing with another. If they say something is something else, even though it is not, they are using a *metaphor*. If they say something is like something else, they are using a *simile*. You probably use metaphors and similes a lot without ever realizing it. Let's say that you tell one of your friends about your 2-year-old brother who bites you when you aren't looking and then runs away laughing: "My little brother is a monster who wants to attack people." You have used a metaphor. Or you say, "My little brother is like a monster who wants to attack people." You have used a simile. Your little brother is bad, but he doesn't really fit the dictionary definition for monster: "A creature with a frightening or bizarre shape or appearance." You have used the term *monster* to convey to your friend that your little brother is a brat when he bites you. He may really be a *brat,* which is a spoiled, bad-mannered child, but he really isn't a grotesquely formed creature that scares people silly, which is what he would be if he were a monster.

Metaphors and similes are often used in poems and stories because they can quickly convey an idea or emotion. In 1849, Henry Wadsworth Longfellow wrote a poem called "The Ship of State." In the poem he uses the metaphor that the United States is a ship. He uses the word *Union* to refer to the ship being a union of states. That is what the name "The United States of America" means. Our country is a whole bunch of states that are united into a country, a union of states. In his poem, where the ship is a metaphor for our country, Longfellow expresses the idea that although our ship of state sometimes sails through rough waters, our ship is strong and sturdy. The poem says that as long as we have faith and hope, and overcome our fears, our ship will continue to sail on. Listen while I read you "The Ship of State."

Read Aloud)))   2. Read to the class:

The Ship of State
Thou, too, sail on, O ship of State!
Sail on, O Union, strong and great!
Humanity with all its fears,
With all the hopes of future years,
Is hanging breathless on thy fate!
We know what Master laid thy keel,
What Workmen wrought thy ribs of steel,
Who made each mast, and sail, and rope,
What anvils rang, and what hammers beat,
In what forge, and what a heat
Were shaped the anchors of thy hope!
Fear not each sudden sound and shock,
'Tis of the wave and not the rock;
'Tis but the flapping of the sail,
And not a rent made by the gale!
In spite of rock and tempest's roar,
In spite of false lights on the shore,
Sail on, nor fear to breast the sea!
Our hearts, our hopes, are all with thee,
Our hearts, our hopes, our prayers, our tears,
Our faith triumphant o'er our fears,
Are all with thee—are all with thee!

3. Tell the students that you want them to copy and try to memorize the first 5 lines of the poem as you write the first 5 lines on the board.

4. After students have completed copying the first 5 lines, erase the lines and have individual students try to recite them from memory (obviously, without looking at their papers).

5. Have students copy the following and give them 5 to 10 minutes to write an answer:

What do you think Henry Wadsworth Longfellow meant when he said in the poem that we should have faith and hope, and not be afraid?

6. Have the students read and discuss their answers or have each student draw a picture about "The Ship of State" or have the students do both.

Exercise 12: "The Flag Goes By"

1. Read to the class:

Have you seen people at a parade or at some event where the flag is either passing by or being posted (put in place)? Many people put their hands over their hearts or take off their hats. Sometimes people do both. By doing these actions, people show respect to the flag and respect for our country. When we show respect to the flag we are showing respect to all of us because we are the country. The flag is a symbol that represents all of us and represents our country. When a country conquers another country, the first thing the conquering country usually does is take down the flag of the country it has just conquered and put up its own flag. This is one reason why people say the flag stands for freedom. When another country's flag is flying over your country and you can no longer fly your own flag, your country is not free. Police officers, rescue workers, military personnel, and firefighters often wear a small American flag patch on their uniforms. The flag is a symbol to show that they are protecting our country, which is all of us.

Our flag flies over government buildings, on ships, and at other places, and a lot of us put it up outside our homes on holidays or at any time just to show we honor and respect our country. When some important person dies or something bad happens, we fly the flag at half-mast to show our respect and sorrow. When a president or a military person dies, the flag is draped over the coffin. Then the flag is carefully folded and given to a surviving relative before the coffin is lowered into the ground. The flag is a final gesture of respect to those who served our country. Sometimes, people don't know what they are supposed to do to show respect to the flag or they forget to show respect. In 1900 Henry Holcomb Bennet wrote a poem reminding people to respect the flag and telling them how to do it. The poem is called "The Flag Goes By."

2. Read to the class:

The Flag Goes By

Hats off!
Along the street there comes
A blare of bugles, a ruffle of drums,
A flash of color beneath the sky:
Hats off!
The flag is passing by!

Blue and crimson and white it shines,
Over the steel-tipped, ordered lines.
Hats off!
The colors before us fly;
But more than the flag is passing by:
Sea-fights and land-fights, grim and great
Fought to make and save the State;
Weary marches and sinking ships;
Cheers of victory on dying lips.

Days of plenty and years of peace;
March of a strong land's swift increase;
Equal justice, right and law,
Stately honor and reverend awe;
Sign of a nation great and strong
To ward her people from foreign wrong;
Pride and glory and honor—all
Live in the colors to stand or fall.

Hats off!
Along the street there comes
A blare of bugles, a ruffle of drums;
And loyal hearts are beating high:
Hats off!
The flag is passing by!

 3. Tell the students you want them to copy and try to memorize the first stanza of the poem as you write the first stanza on the board.

4. After the students have completed copying the first stanza, erase the stanza and have individual students try to recite the stanza from memory (obviously, without looking at their papers).

 5. Have students copy the following and give them 5 to 10 minutes to write an answer:

Should it be illegal to burn the flag as a form of protest? Why or why not?

6. Have the students read their answers to the class and discuss or have each student draw a picture about "The Flag Goes By" or have the students do both.

Exercise 13: Ears

Read Aloud))) 1. Read to the class:

When a pitcher throws a baseball, the catcher catches it. Your ears are your body's catchers of sound waves. A sound is a vibration that your ears are able to catch and pass on to your brain. Your brain is able to recognize the sound if it is something your brain has already placed in its classification system. If it is a sound your brain has not been sent before, your brain will classify the sound according to what is happening at the time and according to what it can associate the sound with from past sounds. Your friend vibrates his vocal chords as he opens his mouth and sends out the word, "Hello." The vibration passes through the air in a fashion similar to an undulating ocean wave. Your ear takes in the vibration and it is passed to your brain, which recognizes the vibration as the word "hello." Another friend is standing next to you and her ears also pick up the vibration and pass it on to her brain, which processes the word as "hello." You create your own vibration by moving your vocal chords to say "Hi" or any of the thousands of vibrations you know how to make.

When we engage in conversation we are experiencing some of the many miracles of the human body. We are sending vibrations and catching vibrations. Conversation is in some ways like a Ping-Pong match between you and someone else, or maybe it is more like a basketball game with players throwing vibrations all over the place. Car engine, airplane overhead, bird chirping, dog barking—your ears pick up vibrations of all kinds to pass on to the brain for decoding. *Warning—danger!* No, the police or fire siren is fading in the distance, having nothing to do with anything near me.

The ear is composed of 3 main sections: the *outer ear,* the *middle ear,* and the *inner ear.* The outer ear has an ear canal through which vibrations pass to the middle ear. Your middle ear has an eardrum that vibrates. The vibrations are passed to the inner ear, where tiny hairs start vibrating. The movement of the hairs sets off nerve impulses that are transmitted to the brain. The brain sorts out the impulses that it has received, identifying the sounds, making you aware of what the sounds are.

Your ears not only catch sounds, they also give you balance. Have you ever heard of or known anyone who because of an ear problem had trouble standing and moving around without being "off-balance"? The inner ear has some little canals that are filled with fluid. When your head moves, the fluid moves, causing nerve endings to send signals to the brain telling the brain what kind of movement is taking place. The brain sends out signals of what to do to maintain balance. If illness or something disrupts the signals between the ear and the brain, the body has difficulty maintaining equilibrium (balance).

As you can tell, the ear is a wonderful part of your body that deserves to be kept in good working order. Loud sounds can damage the ear. People who are in jobs that have a lot of noise may lose hearing, sometimes early in life and sometimes later in life. Loud music, particularly when played directly into the ears, may damage hearing. People who shoot handguns and rifles, particularly police officers and military personnel who frequently spend time on firing ranges, use headgear to protect their ears. Construction workers and others are much more aware today than in the past of the need to wear ear protection when using a jackhammer or doing other jobs that can damage hearing from excessive noise.

2. Have students copy the following:

Ears

Sounds are vibrations in the air.

The vibrations go from the outer ear to the middle ear and then to the inner ear.

The inner ear has little hairs that vibrate and cause signals to be sent to the brain.

The brain decodes the signals, identifying the sounds for us.

The inner ear has small canals that contain fluid that causes signals to be sent to the brain, so that the brain can send signals to tell the body how to maintain balance.

3. Have students copy the following and give them 5 to 10 minutes to write an answer:

Music is popular with most young people, and often they like it loud. How loud is too loud and is listening to the music worth risking hearing loss later in life?

4. Have students read their answers to the class and discuss or have each student draw a picture about ears or have the students do both.

Exercise 14: Eyes

1. Read to the class:

Have you ever had your eyes dilated for an eye examination? Special eyedrops are put into the eyes to cause the pupils to expand and stay open wide. The eye doctor then uses a device called an *opthalmoscope* to put light in 1 eye at a time to look inside it. Normally, the pupils of the eyes would grow smaller to shut out an excessive amount of light, but the special eyedrops make the pupils stay wide open during the exam and usually for a while after the exam is completed. When you are not having your eyes examined, the pupils are expanding and contracting to control the amount of light that is entering the eyes. When you go out in bright sunshine, your pupils get small, to cut down on the amount of light. You go into a darkened room and your pupils get big, to let in as much light as possible. The iris, the part of the eye that gives your eye its color, surrounds the pupil and is made of material that allows the pupil to expand and contract.

When the light has entered the pupil, it then passes through the lens of the eye. If the light is focused correctly as it passes through the lens, the light ends up at the back of the eye on the retina exactly where it should. If the light does not end up where it should you are *nearsighted,* or *farsighted,* or have *astigmatism.* By shifting the focus of the light with glasses, contact lenses, or surgery, the light that enters your eye ends up where it should and you have normal vision.

When light touches the retina at the back of the eye, the light image is converted into nerve impulses that are sent through the optical nerve to the brain. The brain interprets the image and tells us what we are seeing. And by the way, the image that the brain gets is upside down because of the way light rays cross each other in the eye. Of course, your smart brain puts the image right side up for you.

The miracle of sight is just one of the many miracles of our amazing bodies. With such wonderful things as eyes we want to take good care of them and protect them from harm. Our body does much of its own protecting. Over the pupil and iris is the transparent protective cover of the *cornea*. Ever think about how many times your eyelids blink? Your windshield wiper puts moisture on the surface of the eye and keeps it clean by blinking every few seconds. Those eyelashes and eyebrows you have are not just to make you beautiful or handsome. They are protecting your eyes from bright sunlight, dust, and other things that might pose a danger to the eyes. When a lot of dust is blowing around or some danger to the eye is present, your eyelids shut to lock out the danger.

2. Have students copy the following:

   Eyes

   Light passes through the transparent protective covering of the cornea and enters inside the eye through the pupil.

   Pupils dilate or contract to let in more or less light.

   The light passes through the lens of the eye and ends up at the retina in the back of the eye.

   If the light is improperly focused as it passes through the lens, it will not end up where it should be for normal vision.

   Glasses, contacts, or surgery can correctly focus the light, permitting normal vision.

   The light is converted to nerve impulses and sent to the brain to tell us what we are seeing.

3. Have the students copy the following and give them 5 to 10 minutes to write an answer:

   What are the differences between a blink and a wink, and what could happen if somebody thought a blink was a wink?

4. Have students read their answers to the class and discuss or have each student draw a picture about eyes or have the students do both.

Exercise 15: Teeth

1. Read to the class:

When you were born you didn't have any teeth unless you were one of the few babies who has a tooth at birth. Like most babies you probably got your first tooth at around 6 to 8 months, or maybe a little later. As more teeth started popping up, you got a little cranky or maybe even very cranky. When the teething was all over by the time you were 2 or 3 years old, you were probably very comfortable with your set of 20 baby teeth. But instead of the baby teeth growing into big teeth, other teeth started pushing up when you were about 6 years old, making the baby teeth get loose. The baby teeth fell out, unless you pulled them out when they got loose. To make the changeover of teeth a little fun, maybe you were lucky enough to have someone tell you that the "tooth fairy" would leave you a little money or something nice each time you lost a tooth. This time you would get a set of 32 new teeth, unless you didn't get all 4 wisdom teeth, which some people don't. They are called *wisdom teeth* because they arrive later than the other teeth, and it is assumed that since you are older you are wiser. By the age of 12, usually earlier, most people have a full set of teeth except for the wisdom teeth, which may still be a few years away from arriving at the back of the rows of teeth.

Your permanent teeth, as they are now called, have arrived in four types: incisors, canines, premolars, and molars. The front teeth are *incisors,* sharp, thin teeth that bite into something and hold on. Behind the incisors are the *canine teeth,* which can rip into something the way a dog might tear at a piece of meat, thus the name canine teeth. The upper canine teeth are also called *eye teeth* because of their location, like eyes in the front of your mouth. Then come the *premolars,* also called *bicuspids.* They are wider, with an edge around the outside and an indentation at the center of each tooth. Then come the *molars,* the big heavy teeth that chomp apart the food to prepare it for its journey to your stomach.

As you look at your teeth in the mirror you may decide that there was an error in their placement, because some of them were set in at the wrong angle. Teeth like these are commonly called crooked teeth. Lucky you if you have crooked teeth; it's time for braces, either the kind that extends over many teeth and stays in your mouth maybe even for a year or 2, or the kind that doesn't cover much area and can be removed frequently. While you are getting your teeth pushed around by the dentist, you hear some more about proper dental care, a subject you have heard many times: brush and floss, and see your dentist every 6 months or once a year. Your dentist sends you out into the world of good dental care, but a couple of years later you have to have a tooth filled. Maybe you didn't always remember to brush and floss well after eating. The bacteria in your mouth built up and formed plaque. The plaque worked its way into your teeth, eating away at it. With your tooth filled you leave the dental office, vowing to do all of the things you need to do to take good care of your teeth.

2. Have students copy the following:

Teeth

The 20 baby teeth are replaced by about 32 permanent teeth.

The permanent teeth consist of incisors, canines, premolars (bicuspids), and molars.

Wisdom teeth arrive much later than the other teeth and not everyone gets all 4 wisdom teeth.

Tooth decay is caused by bacteria forming plaque that eats away at the tooth.

Brushing, flossing, and regular trips to the dentist can prevent the buildup of plaque.

3. Have students copy the following and give them 5 to 10 minutes to write an answer:

What are some of the difficulties of having braces and would it be worth having braces if only 1 tooth or 2 teeth are out of place?

4. Have students read their answers to the class and discuss or have each student draw a picture about teeth or have the students do both.

Exercise 16: Skin and Hair

1. Read to the class:

Your body is *endothermic,* which means that you are *warm-blooded.* Birds and mammals fit into this category. Fish, amphibians, and reptiles are *ectothermic,* which means they are *cold-blooded.* Warm-blooded creatures maintain a constant temperature in the body; in the case of humans it is about 98.6 degrees Fahrenheit. When your temperature goes up even a few degrees it is usually an indication that you are ill. The body temperature of cold-blooded creatures fluctuates according to how hot or cold it is outside the body. The body temperature of a lizard on a rock during the day is much higher than at night when the sun goes down. Your skin helps maintain your constant body temperature. Signals pass between the skin and brain to let the skin know what it must do to help maintain a 98.6 degree temperature. Your skin will perspire to help cool you down on a hot day. When you get cold, the blood vessels near your skin constrict (become narrower), helping to keep warmth from escaping through your skin. When you are very cold, your muscles tighten in what we call *shivering,* which produces heat to try to warm you up.

Your skin is, obviously, the covering for the outside of your body. The outer later of skin is called the *epidermis.* Under the *epidermis* is a layer called the *dermis.* Hairs stick down through the epidermis and the dermis and are anchored in a fatty layer called the *hypodermis.* Humans, as well as other mammals, have hair or fur. Birds also share the characteristic of having hair (feathers), because they are warm-blooded and need feathers to keep them warm when temperatures are cold. Ever think about how ducks and geese are able to withstand the cold water temperatures and maintain their body heat? Could body fat and feathers have something to do with it?

A normal human hair will grow for about 3 years and then fall out, being replaced by another hair. The average person loses more than 100 hairs a day. The average young adult has about 100,000 hairs on the head so that hair loss is usually of no concern. Hair becomes thinner (less in quantity) and gets grayer as people grow older. About 40 percent of people are turning gray or are gray by the time they are 40 years old. About two-thirds of men will show some degree of baldness by the age of 60, the amount of baldness differing with individuals. Women tend to lose their hair in an overall pattern, becoming thinner over the entire head rather than becoming totally bald in a particular spot. Some men have a "watermelon rind" of hair on the sides and back, with the top being totally bald; others have a receding hairline in the front and perhaps a bald spot at the top back. Others have the bowling ball look of total baldness.

As you know, hair is cut without any pain. Hair is made of *keratin,* which is the same protein that composes your nails. Cutting skin sets off a pain alarm, but skin is pretty tough and has the amazing capacity to zip up the wound. Signals travel between the brain and the skin, and the body springs into action repairing the damage.

There are all kinds of skin disorders that people get. An inflammation of the skin is referred to as *dermatitis* and a medical doctor who specializes in treating skin problems is a *dermatologist. Acne* is very common among adolescents, with about three-fourths of teenagers having some degree of the skin problem. Extreme cases are the exception rather than the rule. Teenage boys have a greater incidence of acne than girls do. Fortunately, acne usually lessens or completely disappears in adulthood.

2. Have students copy the following:

   Skin and Hair

   Humans are endothermic (warm-blooded) and maintain a normal body temperature of 98.6 degrees Fahrenheit.

   Skin helps maintain a normal body temperature by constricting blood vessels, sweating, tightening muscles, and shivering.

   A human hair usually grows for about 3 years before falling out and being replaced by another hair.

   Men and women usually lose hair and become gray as they grow older.

   About three-fourths of teenagers have some degree of acne.

   Acne usually diminishes or completely disappears in adulthood.

3. Have students copy the following and give them 5 to 10 minutes to write an answer:

   Should you be embarrassed about any of the following: hair, skin color, height, age, acne? Explain your answer.

4. Have students read their answers to the class and discuss or have each student draw a picture about the skin or hair (or both) or have students do both.

Exercise 17: Richard Nixon

1. Read to the class:

When Richard Nixon was sworn in as president on January 20, 1969, the nation was at war in Vietnam. Under President Lyndon Johnson, the man Nixon replaced as president, the United States had gone to the aid of noncommunist South Vietnam as it tried to defend itself against communist North Vietnam. President Johnson had been unable to bring the war to a successful conclusion even with over a half-million Americans fighting on the side of South Vietnam. President

Johnson had decided not to run for reelection. Richard Nixon ran against Hubert Humphrey and was elected. This was not the first time Richard Nixon had run for president. After 2 terms as vice president under President Eisenhower, Nixon had run against John Kennedy in 1960. Kennedy had won a narrow victory and it was not until 8 years later that Nixon had again secured the nomination of the Republican Party and this time was victorious.

President Nixon wanted to bring about what he called "peace with honor" in Vietnam. His plan was to try to get the communist countries of China and the Soviet Union, who supported communist North Vietnam, to encourage North Vietnam to stop waging war on South Vietnam. President Nixon established a policy of *détente,* which meant trying to get along with the Soviet Union and China even if they were communist countries while keeping our military strong enough to keep China and the Soviet Union from attacking us or trying to take over other countries. President Nixon visited China in 1972, reestablishing diplomatic contact between the U.S. and China, which had ended in 1949 when the Chinese civil war had concluded in a communist victory. To get American troops out of Vietnam, President Nixon came up with a plan called *Vietnamization.* This plan was to build up the military strength of South Vietnam and gradually withdraw American troops while turning more of the fighting over to the South Vietnamese.

By the time President Nixon was reelected in 1972, most American troops had been withdrawn from Vietnam. Around Christmas of 1972 the United States bombed selected targets in Hanoi, the capital of North Vietnam. The North Vietnamese agreed to a peace settlement in 1973 and released Americans who had been captured during the war. Many of the Americans were pilots who had been shot down during the war and held in North Vietnamese prisons, where they were tortured and treated brutally by North Vietnamese prison guards. President Nixon had overwhelmingly won the election of 1972 and it seemed that his second term was off to a good start.

During the campaign for president, a small group of men connected to President Nixon's reelection campaign had broken into the Democratic Party headquarters in the Watergate complex of buildings in Washington, D.C. They had been caught in an apparent attempt to go through files of the Democratic Party. President Nixon may or may not have ordered the break-in, but he tried to cover up what had happened; in other words, he did not want to provide any information that would help in prosecuting the burglars or having them associated with his reelection campaign.

The president has a duty to see that the laws of the United States are enforced. There was an investigation and the United States House of Representatives brought impeachment charges against President Nixon, charging him with obstruction of justice, abuse of power, and contempt of Congress. Before the United States Senate could put him on trial, President Nixon resigned as president at noon on August 9, 1974. A surprised nation watched on television as former President Nixon and close family members boarded a helicopter and flew away from the White House.

Vice President Gerald Ford was immediately sworn in as president. Nixon was disgraced, and his reputation suffered accordingly. But by the time he died on April 22, 1994, his reputation had been restored somewhat by the knowledge he had on how to deal with other countries. He was often asked to make speeches and give advice on foreign affairs.

2. Have students copy the following:

Richard Nixon (1913–1994)

Thirty-seventh president (1969–1974)

In 1968 when Richard Nixon won the presidential election, over a half-million Americans were fighting in Vietnam.

By the time he won reelection in 1972, most American troops had been withdrawn from Vietnam.

In 1973 communist North Vietnam signed a peace agreement and freed American prisoners of war.

During President Nixon's reelection campaign in 1972, some men broke into the Democratic Party headquarters at the Watergate complex.

President Nixon tried to obstruct the investigation of the Watergate break-in.

The U.S. House of Representatives brought impeachment charges against him.

Nixon resigned as president on August 9, 1974, before the U.S. Senate could put him on trial.

3. Have students copy the following and give them 5 to 10 minutes to write an answer:

President Andrew Johnson in 1868 and President Bill Clinton in 1998 were impeached by the House of Representatives but both were acquitted in trials by the Senate. Explain whether or not you think it would have been better for President Nixon to have stood trial in the Senate than to resign.

4. Have students read their answers to the class and discuss or have each student draw a picture about Richard Nixon or have the students do both.

Exercise 18: Gerald Ford

1. Read to the class:

Gerald Ford was sworn in as president on August 9, 1974. President Ford then chose Nelson Rockefeller to be his vice president. For the first time in our nation's history, neither the president nor the vice president had been elected to office. Gerald Ford had been chosen by President Nixon to be his new vice president when Nixon's first vice president, Spiro Agnew, resigned. Then when Nixon resigned, Ford moved up to president and chose his vice president, Nelson Rockefeller.

Although President Ford had not been elected to his new office, he had a lot of experience in being elected to office. He had served 24 years in the U.S. House of Representatives. All members run for the office every 2 years. Gerald Ford had been a football hero in high school and college. After completing law school he had been an officer in the U.S. Navy during World War II. In 1948, Ford had been elected to the House of Representatives, starting his first term in 1949 and serving there until 1973, when he had been picked to be vice president by Richard Nixon.

Gerald Ford was greatly respected and trusted as the leader of the Republicans in the House, so he entered the office of president in 1974 with most people liking him and thinking he would be a good president. He knew that he had to restore confidence in the government. He needed to reassure the American people that even though a vice president and then a president had resigned after being accused of wrongdoing that the government was honest and would continue to function.

The U.S. Constitution gives the president the "power to grant reprieves and pardons for offenses against the United States." A month after President Nixon resigned from office, President Ford pardoned him for any crimes he might have committed while president. This meant that the former president could not be tried in any court for anything he might have done in connection with the Watergate break-in. President Ford said he issued the pardon to get the whole Watergate episode behind the nation, so that the country didn't have to go through the ordeal of seeing a former president tried in a regular court for being an accomplice in a burglary or some other criminal charge. Some people thought the pardon was a good thing; others were very angry at President Ford for giving Nixon the pardon.

While the controversy over Watergate and President Nixon's resignation and pardon was going on, North Vietnam decided to break the peace agreement that had been made in 1973. North Vietnam was again attacking South Vietnam. President Ford, members of Congress, and most Americans did not want to see Americans again fighting in Vietnam. Approximately 58,000 Americans had been killed fighting the North Vietnamese communists before the peace agreement had been signed in 1973. Now, 2 years later, it looked like the amount of military aid being sent to South Vietnam would have to be increased and American troops would be needed again if North Vietnam was to be stopped from taking over South Vietnam.

President Ford said in a speech on April 23, 1975, that the war in Vietnam was finished. U.S. military forces evacuated Americans who were in South Vietnam along with many South Vietnamese as communist North Vietnam troops overran South Vietnam. The fall of South Vietnam was so swift, that among many of those who were trying to get evacuated a state of panic existed. So many helicopters brought so many people to U.S. ships that some helicopters were pushed overboard into the sea to make room for more helicopters to land. Many South Vietnamese got on whatever boats they could find and tried to sail away from Vietnam. Many South Vietnamese eventually came to the United States and became U.S. citizens.

When President Gerald Ford ran against Jimmy Carter in the 1976 presidential election, Jimmy Carter was elected president by a narrow margin. President Ford had served the nation in a difficult time. He served when Americans needed to have faith in their government restored after a vice president and a president had resigned because of charges of wrongdoing. President Ford served when the United States was faced with the difficult decisions of whether or not to increase military aid to South Vietnam and send American troops to again fight in Vietnam.

2. Have students copy the following:

Gerald Ford (1913–)

Thirty-eighth president (1974–1977)

Vice President Ford became president when President Nixon resigned.

President Ford pardoned Nixon for any crimes he might have committed while president.

Communist North Vietnam violated the peace agreement made in 1973 and again started attacking South Vietnam.

The United States decided not to increase the amount of military aid being sent to South Vietnam and not to send American troops to again fight in Vietnam.

Many South Vietnamese were evacuated to American ships as communist forces were overrunning South Vietnam.

South Vietnam was taken over in 1975 by communist North Vietnam.

Many South Vietnamese who had escaped Vietnam on American ships and other boats eventually became U.S. citizens.

3. Have students copy the following and give them 5 to 10 minutes to write an answer:

Presidents and governors have the power to pardon people. Explain why you think this is a good or bad thing.

4. Have students read their answers to the class and discuss or have each student draw a picture about Gerald Ford or have the students do both.

Exercise 19: Jimmy Carter

1. Read to the class:

When Jimmy Carter was born on October 1, 1924, in Plains, Georgia, he was named James Earl Carter Jr. He preferred being called "Jimmy," and by the time he became president in 1977, Jimmy Carter was his official name. In 2002, long after he had been president, he was awarded a Nobel Peace Prize. The prize was awarded largely for what he did as president, when he got Egypt and Israel to sign a peace agreement to help them get along with each other.

In that same year, 1979, President Carter was unable to solve a crisis between the United States and the country of Iran. The crisis dragged on through the entire year of 1980 and did not end until Ronald Reagan was sworn in as president on January 20, 1981. President Carter, on January 19, 1981, agreed to some of the demands that Iran had made. Whether it was Carter's agreeing to some of Iran's demands, Reagan taking office, a combination of both, or some other factors, the crisis finally ended on January 20, 1981.

The crisis had begun on November 4, 1979, when Iranians stormed the U.S. Embassy in Tehran, the capital city of Iran. The Iranians captured 90 people, 66 of them Americans. Eventually, some of the hostages were released, with 52 Americans remaining in captivity. The United States and Iran were not at war, and President Carter did not want to go to war. The Iranians said they had seized the hostages to protest the former leader of Iran, Shah Mohammed Reza Pahlavi, being in the United States for medical treatment for cancer. They demanded that the United States turn the Shah over to them. The new leader of Iran, Ayatollah Khomeini, said that unless the Shah returned to Iran, some of the hostages would be put on trial as spies.

The United States did not arrest the Shah and send him to Iran. Iranians burned American flags, paraded blindfolded captives in front of TV cameras, and shouted condemnations of the United States. The Ayatollah Khomeini called the United States "the Great Satan." When the Shah had been deposed as ruler of Iran, Iran had set up a theocracy, in this case a religious government run by the religion of Islam, with the Ayatollah Khomeini being both the political and religious leader of the country. The crisis dragged on month after month, with Americans still held hostage in Iran.

On April 24, 1980, President Carter sent a small military force in helicopters to try to rescue the hostages. The helicopters turned back before they reached Tehran. The rescue was a complete failure, with sandstorms in the desert causing some of the helicopters to crash, killing 8 Americans. The Shah left the United States and died from his cancer while in Egypt. After 444 days of being held captive in Iran, the hostages were released about 6 months after the Shah died. President Carter had avoided going to war with Iran, but many Americans were unhappy with how he had handled the Iranian hostage crisis.

Some of the other actions that President Carter took were very controversial but not as unpopular as his handling of the hostage crisis. Some people agreed and some people didn't agree when he pardoned Vietnam draft evaders. *Draft evaders* were American men who refused to go into the military when drafted during the Vietnam War. Some fled to Canada, some hid out, some went to jail rather than serve in the military.

Some people thought President Carter's decision to turn over the Panama Canal to Panama was the fair thing to do. Others thought it was a terrible decision because the United States, at great cost in money and construction workers' lives, had built the canal, had opened it to ship traffic in 1914, and had operated it ever since. President Carter negotiated a treaty that would gradually turn the Panama Canal over to Panama. The final phase of the transfer of the canal to Panama was completed in the year 2000.

President Carter also made the decision to boycott the 1980 Olympics in Moscow because the Soviet Union had invaded Afghanistan. Athletes who had trained for years to be in the Olympics and others who thought sports should not be used for political purposes were very unhappy about the United States not being a part of the Summer Olympics.

President Carter was easily defeated by Ronald Reagan in the 1980 presidential election. After leaving office Jimmy Carter contributed a great deal of his time to humanitarian work, helping to build houses for poor people and doing other charitable works.

2. Have students copy the following:

Jimmy Carter (1924–)

Thirty-ninth president (1977–1981)

He got Israel and Egypt to sign a peace treaty.

He pardoned Vietnam draft evaders.

He signed a treaty to give the Panama Canal to Panama.

He had the U.S. boycott the 1980 Summer Olympics to protest the Soviet Union's invasion of Afghanistan.

Americans were held hostage in Iran for 444 days after Iranians took over the American Embassy in Tehran.

American hostages were released on January 20, 1981, when President Reagan was sworn in as the new president.

3. Have students copy the following and give them 5 to 10 minutes to write an answer:

Should the Olympics ever be boycotted? Explain why you think they should or should not ever be boycotted.

4. Have students read their answers to the class and discuss or have each student draw a picture about Jimmy Carter or have students do both.

Exercise 20: Ronald Reagan

Read Aloud

1. Read to the class:

In 1980 the rate of inflation in the United States was about 13 percent, which meant that, on average, what Americans had paid a dollar for in 1979 they had to pay $1.13 for in 1980. The unemployment rate in 1980 was over 7 percent, which meant that out of every 100 Americans, 7 were unemployed. This was not nearly as high as the unemployment rate had been during the Great Depression of the 1930s, but it was high for normal times. Many Americans were not happy with the nation's economy. For 444 days Americans had been held hostage in Iran with President Carter sending a military rescue mission that failed miserably. The U.S. military seemed to be in a state of decline since the end of the Vietnam War and many Americans were despondent over what seemed to be America's declining influence in the world.

In the 1980 presidential race most Americans were willing to give Ronald Reagan the chance to do something different and overwhelmingly elected him. Ronald Reagan received 43,899,248 votes to Jimmy Carter's 35,481,435 votes, which gave Reagan 489 electoral votes to Carter's 49 electoral votes. Four years later in the election of 1984 Reagan would win reelection by an even larger margin, getting 525 electoral votes to Walter Mondale's 13 electoral votes.

Ronald Reagan had been a movie and TV actor most of his adult working life. He was so good at public speaking that when he entered politics and became governor of California and later president he was nicknamed "the Great Communicator." Reagan came into office with set ideas on what the government should do, and during his 8 years as president those ideas were put into effect. He wanted to rebuild America's military might and restore America's sense of confidence in its military. He wanted to cut taxes, cut some welfare and social programs, and have Americans rely less on government and more on themselves. He wanted to give businesses more freedom to operate and invest to create jobs.

By the end of his time as president he had achieved most of his major goals but there were a few setbacks and problems. In relations with foreign countries President Reagan achieved great success in being tough and standing up to the Soviet Union, and then working cooperatively with the Soviet Union to lessen tensions and achieve better understanding between the United States and the Soviet Union. American military forces were sent to various places around the world to maintain peace or to further American interests, usually without harm to American troops. One exception was the country of Lebanon, where a suicide terrorist crashed a truck loaded with explosives into a U.S. Marine barracks, killing 241 Americans.

The American economy picked up steam under Reagan's tax cuts when some strict government regulations on businesses were ended. Unemployment went up during President Reagan's first year in office, but both unemployment and inflation had dropped significantly by the end of his term in office. The national debt remained high, but that did not seem to have much effect on the nation's economy. With the economy in good shape, with people working and prices rising some, but not much, President Reagan was still very popular with most Americans.

Americans felt good about the military being strong and respected in the world and they were relieved that the United States and the Soviet Union were getting along with each other much better. President Reagan's time in office seemed to be an overwhelming success without much going wrong.

Then came the "Iran-Contra scandal," which caused some people not to think as highly of the Reagan administration as they had. In 1987 it was learned that some people in President Reagan's administration had possibly violated laws by selling military arms to Iran to get hostages released. The money made from the sale of the military weapons to Iran was given to anticommunist forces in the country of Nicaragua who were fighting communist forces for control of the Nicaraguan government. Hearings in Congress went on for months, but no charges were ever brought against President Reagan. Some of those directly involved in selling weapons to Iran and giving the money to the anticommunist forces fighting in Nicaragua were charged with offenses and convicted. On appeal some of the convictions were thrown out.

President Reagan ended his 8 years in office at the age of 77, which was older than any other president had been. He had been shot by a mentally deranged man a few months after entering office. The deranged man thought that by shooting the president he would win the love of a famous movie actress. President Reagan survived the serious wound, served out the rest of that term and then served a second term. He lived until 2004, dying at the age of 93.

2. Have students copy the following:

Ronald Reagan (1911–2004)

Fortieth president (1981–1989)

He built up the military, reduced taxes, did away with some government regulations on business, and cut some government programs.

The inflation rate and the unemployment rate went down.

A suicide terrorist in Lebanon crashed a truck loaded with explosives into a U.S. Marine barracks, killing 241 Americans.

Reagan was never charged in the Iran-Contra scandal, but some of those in his administration were.

3. Have students copy the following and give them 5 to 10 minutes to write an answer:

The U.S. Constitution states that to become president a person has to be at least 35 years old and have been born a U.S. citizen. Explain whether or not you think the U.S. Constitution should be amended to change or add to these requirements.

4. Have students read their answers to the class and discuss or have each student draw a picture about Ronald Reagan or have the students do both.

Exercise 21: The Statue of Liberty, Mount Rushmore

1. Say to the class: "Two of the most famous monuments in the United States are the Statue of Liberty and Mount Rushmore. Number your sheet of paper from 1 to 20. Then, for each item I read, write either 'SL' for Statue of Liberty or 'MR' for Mount Rushmore. If you don't know an answer, guess."

2. Read the following items to the class, without reading the answers that are in parentheses:

(1) Designed by Gutzon Borglum (MR).

(2) Designed by Frédéric Auguste Bartholdi (SL).

(3) George Washington (MR; one of the presidents on MR).

(4) Granite (MR carved out of granite).

(5) Gift from France (SL).

(6) Dedicated in 1886 (SL).

(7) Dedicated in 1927 (MR).

(8) Work to create the monument continued for many years after the monument was dedicated (MR).

(9) Designer of the monument died before the monument could be completed (MR; Gutzon Borglum died in 1941 and his son took over for a while; monument was never totally completed as Gutzon Borglum had wanted it completed).

(10) Monument went through 4 years of restoration before its centennial (100-year) celebrations in 1986 (SL).

(11) President during the Civil War (MR; Lincoln is one of the presidents on MR).

(12) Grover Cleveland (SL; president who dedicated SL in 1886).

(13) The name "Bedloe's Island" was changed to "Liberty Island" in 1956 (SL; island where SL stands).

(14) Calvin Coolidge (MR; president who dedicated MR in 1927).

(15) More closely associated with immigrants (SL; immigrants saw SL on their way to Ellis Island).

(16) Dynamite and jackhammers were used for many years (MR; things used to carve figures on MR).

(17) Had to be assembled piece by metal piece (SL; statue arrived in pieces in crates from France).

(18) "The New Colossus" (SL; title of poem engraved on pedestal that SL stands on).

(19) Black Hills (MR; mountains in South Dakota where MR is).

(20) "Father of Our Country," author of the Declaration of Independence, president when U.S. became a world leader, preserved the Union while doing away with slavery (MR; George Washington, Thomas Jefferson, Theodore Roosevelt, Abraham Lincoln).

3. Have each student check his or her own paper as you read the item again, this time along with the answer that is in parentheses.

4. Say to the class: "Emma Lazarus was the lady who wrote the poem 'The New Colossus,' which is engraved at the base of the Statue of Liberty. I am going to write the last part of the poem on the board and I want you to copy it. This is the most famous part of the poem."

The New Colossus, by Emma Lazarus

Give me your tired, your poor,
Your huddled masses yearning to breathe free,
The wretched refuse of your teeming shore.
Send these, the homeless, tempest-tost to me,
I lift my lamp beside the golden door!

5. Have students copy the following and give them 5 to 10 minutes to write an answer:

Why do people create monuments and why do you think the monuments of the Statue of Liberty and Mount Rushmore were created?

6. Have students read their answers to the class and discuss or have each student draw a picture about the Statue of Liberty or Mount Rushmore (or both) or have students do both.

Exercise 22: George Herbert Walker Bush

Read Aloud)))   1. Read to the class:

When George Herbert Walker Bush became president in 1989 he was usually referred to as "President Bush" or "President George Bush." When his son, George Walker Bush, became president in 2001, there had to be a way of distinguishing between father and son. The elder Bush is sometimes referred to as "George H. W. Bush." The son is sometimes referred to as "George W. Bush" or just "George W." Another common way to tell the difference between the 2 is "George Bush (41)" and "George Bush (43)," since the father was the forty-first president and the son became the forty-third president. John Adams, the second president, and his son, the sixth president, had a similar problem. The problem was easily remedied by always referring to the father as "John Adams" and the son as "John Quincy Adams," using the son's middle name as well as first name.

George H. W. Bush became a U.S. Navy pilot in World War II when he was not yet out of his teens. His plane was shot down by the Japanese and he was rescued from the ocean by a U.S. submarine that was on the surface. Many years later when he became president he was very experienced in government jobs. He had been a member of Congress, U.S. ambassador to the United Nations, representative of the U.S. to China, head of the Central Intelligence Agency, and President Reagan's vice president for 2 terms.

President Reagan's policies, world events, and the Soviet economy had led to a Soviet Union that was having difficulty controlling the countries of Eastern Europe that it had taken over during World War II. During George H. W. Bush's term as president the Berlin Wall came down and the Soviet Union pulled out of Eastern Europe. Parts of the Soviet Union broke away and became independent countries. What was left of the Soviet Union went back to its old name, Russia, and abandoned communism.

Meanwhile, in the Middle East in 1990, the dictator of Iraq, Saddam Hussein, launched an attack on Kuwait, Iraq's neighbor, and captured it. President Bush (41) assembled a coalition of countries to restore Kuwait's independence, and they attacked Saddam's military forces in January and February 1991. After a month of missile strikes from ships and air attacks by mostly American and British airplanes, Iraq's troops were forced out of Kuwait in a ground war that lasted only 100 hours. President Bush (41), to stop the killing, ordered a halt to the war since Kuwait was once again an independent country. Iraq's army had been driven back into Iraq and it was thought that Saddam Hussein and Iraq would not again be a threat to Middle East peace. President George H. W. Bush's popularity soared after the quick victory over Iraq's army, which had been regarded as one of the strongest in the world.

President Bush (41) had done what most people thought was an excellent job of handling foreign affairs. Eastern Europe was once again free. The Soviet Union had broken up and given up communism. Kuwait was again an independent country. There had even been a small successful U.S. military invasion into the country of Panama on December 20, 1989, to arrest General Manuel Antonio Noriega, who was thought to be trafficking in drugs and turning Panama into a dictatorship.

But while President Bush (41) had been focusing on foreign affairs, the United States at home had slipped into a recession, which is when the economy slows down and some people lose jobs. Presidential candidate Bill Clinton in his campaign repeatedly pointed out the bad news about the economy. President George H. W. Bush's popularity dropped. In addition to the bad economy, President Bush (41) had made the promise not to raise taxes, but he had broken his promise. Bill Clinton won the election and became president on January 20, 1993, even though there were signs that the economy was improving and coming out of the recession.

2. Have students copy the following:

George Herbert Walker Bush (1924–)

Forty-first president

The Soviet Union pulled out of Europe, gave up communism, and went back to its old name of "Russia" when parts of it broke away to become independent countries.

Iraq invaded Kuwait and conquered it.

President Bush (41) organized American, British, and other military forces to free Kuwait.

Iraq was expelled from Kuwait after a month of air bombardment and 100 hours of ground war.

President Bush (41) became very popular after winning the war so quickly, but became unpopular over the economy.

He was defeated by Bill Clinton in the 1992 presidential election.

3. Have students copy the following and give them 5 to 10 minutes to write an answer:

Explain why you think the United States should or should not ever go to war to free a country or to keep another country from being conquered.

4. Have students read their answers to the class and discuss or draw a picture about George Herbert Walker Bush or do both.

Exercise 23: Bill Clinton

1. Read to the class:

When Bill Clinton became president on January 20, 1993, the economy was coming out of a recession. During his administration, the economy continued to prosper. In general, the U.S. was in a time of peace and prosperity during his years in office. Most people were satisfied with the way things were going in the country and he was reelected to a second 4-year term. Nevertheless, Bill Clinton became the second president in U.S. history to be put on trial by the U.S. Senate.

Bill Clinton had been born William Jefferson Blythe on August 19, 1946, having been named for his father. His father had died in an automobile accident before Bill was born. When Bill was 16 years old his last name was changed to Clinton, the same last name as that of his mother and stepfather. By the time he became president at the age of 46, the name he preferred was Bill, and so he was Bill Clinton.

Outside of some squabbles with Congress, which is normal for a president, he seemed to be having a successful time in office when he started his second term. Then came the "Monica Lewinsky scandal." Although President Clinton was nearly 50 years old and had been married for twenty years to Hillary Rodham Clinton, he began meeting secretly with a 21-year-old woman named Monica Lewinsky. She had come to Washington, D.C., to learn about our government by working as an intern. The president eventually refused to meet with her anymore, and she was transferred from her job at the White House to a job at the Pentagon.

Rumors about their relationship circulated and, as often happens with matters that people try to keep secret, some people found out. An investigation was held and led to impeachment charges being brought by the House of Representatives against the president. President Clinton had not wanted to cooperate with the investigation, so he was accused of obstructing justice. He had denied that he had been involved with Monica Lewinsky, so he was charged with *perjury,* which is lying under oath. It takes two-thirds of the 100 senators voting guilty to remove a president from office. Two-thirds of 100 senators requires 67 senators to vote guilty in order to convict. In President Clinton's trial in the Senate in 1999, the vote on the charge of obstructing justice was 50 for not guilty and 50 for guilty; on the charge of perjury the vote was 55 for not guilty and 45 for guilty. He was not removed from office.

Bill Clinton served out the rest of his term, which had almost 2 years to go and ended when George W. Bush was sworn into office on January 20, 2001. President Clinton apologized to the American people on TV. His wife, Hillary Rodham Clinton, stayed married to him, and in 2001 she became a U.S. senator from the state of New York. Monica Lewinsky was a celebrity for a while and then, as interest in her waned, she returned to a more private life.

2. Have students copy the following:

Bill Clinton (1946–)

Forty-second president (1993–2001)

The country generally enjoyed peace and prosperity during his time in office.

President Clinton had an affair with Monica Lewinsky, a 21-year-old intern at the White House.

An investigation took place and the House of Representatives charged President Clinton with perjury and obstructing justice.

The trial in the U.S. Senate did not get the necessary two-thirds vote for guilty to convict President Clinton of either charge and remove him from office.

3. Have the students copy the following and give them 5 to 10 minutes to write an answer:

Explain why you think what a president does in his or her private life should or should not be of concern to anybody, so long as no laws are broken.

4. Have students read their answers to the class and discuss or draw a picture about Bill Clinton or do both.

Exercise 24: George Walker Bush

Read Aloud

1. Read to the class:

The presidential election of 2000 was one of the most contested in United States history. Democratic candidate Al Gore, who had been vice president under Bill Clinton, got slightly more popular votes than Republican George Walker Bush, but Bush got more electoral votes, making him president. The final electoral vote count was 271 for Bush and 266 for Gore. President George W. Bush or Bush (43), to distinguish him from his father George H. W. Bush or Bush (41) who had also been president, plunged right into work as president. He came into office promising tax cuts and other things he wanted to get done in what is called the "domestic agenda," as distinct from "foreign affairs." But almost 9 months into his presidency he was forced to shift his attention from his domestic agenda to foreign terrorists.

On September 11, 2001, terrorists crashed 2 hijacked airliners into the twin towers of the World Trade Center in New York City. Another hijacked airliner crashed into the Pentagon in Washington, D.C. A fourth hijacked airliner was on its way to crash into another target in Washington, D.C., but it crashed into the ground in Pennsylvania, probably as a result of passengers on the plane struggling with the hijackers for control of the plane. Everybody on all 4 airliners was killed, as were over 100 people at the Pentagon, and about 2,500 people at the World Trade Center, including some of the firefighters and police officers who rushed into the buildings to rescue people.

With about 3,000 people dead in the attacks, President Bush (43) quickly went after the Taliban rulers and Al Qaeda terrorist organization in the country of Afghanistan who were thought to be responsible for the attacks. U.S. military forces, aided by allies, mainly the British, captured Afghanistan. The Taliban rulers were deposed and a temporary leader was appointed until the country could be made safe enough to hold elections. The temporary leader, Hamid Karzai, was elected president. Osama bin Laden, a leader of the terrorists, remained at large, with U.S. and other forces looking for him, mainly in the area between Afghanistan and Pakistan.

President Bush (43) and Congress created a Department of Homeland Security to better protect Americans from terrorists. All kinds of new security measures went into effect. Airports and other places where terrorists might attack started to check people more closely and took other measures to prevent attacks.

Saddam Hussein, the dictator of Iraq, had been thought to no longer be a threat to other countries after President Bush (41) successfully sent American, British, and other troops to defeat Saddam Hussein's army and ejected Iraq from the neighboring country of Kuwait almost 10 years earlier. As a condition of peace, Saddam Hussein was not to make or possess chemical, biological, and nuclear weapons. Intelligence reports said that Saddam Hussein had the forbidden weapons of mass destruction. He also ignored numerous resolutions of the United Nations.

President Bush (43) and Prime Minister Tony Blair of Great Britain sent forces to Iraq to disarm Saddam Hussein's army. U.S., British, and small numbers of troops from other countries won a quick victory in Iraq. The weapons of mass destruction were not found, but torture rooms, mass graves, and evidence of beatings showed the brutality of Saddam Hussein's regime. It was also known that Saddam Hussein had used chemical weapons on some of his own people. Saddam Hussein could not be found when Baghdad, the capital city, was captured. The hunt for him went on for many months and he was finally captured hiding in a "spider hole," a small underground room.

Although Saddam Hussein's army had been defeated, terrorists started attacking American and British forces. The attacks progressed to attacks on the military forces of any country in Iraq, then to anyone trying to help rebuild the country, including Iraqis. The weapons they used were often suicide car bombers, roadside bombs, and rocket-propelled grenades. Terrorists also kidnapped a lot of people, beheading many of them or killing them by other means. A temporary Iraqi government had been installed and terrorists were trying to prevent an election that would elect leaders and set up a democratic government in Iraq. After the election, they continued their violent attempts to disrupt the new government.

In 2004 the U.S. held another presidential election. The election, like the one in 2000, was bitterly fought. President Bush (43) was reelected, this time winning both the popular vote and the electoral vote to defeat John Kerry. President Bush (43) continued to work on achieving the goals he had established during his first term in office. He also continued to work to stop terrorists from killing innocent people in Iraq and elsewhere in the world.

2. Have students copy the following:

George Walker Bush (1946–)

Forty-third president (2001–)

On September 11, 2001, terrorists attacked the World Trade Center and the Pentagon, killing a lot of people.

President Bush (43) and Congress established the Department of Homeland Security.

U.S., British, and military forces from other countries defeated the Taliban rulers and terrorists in Afghanistan.

U.S., British, and other military forces defeated Saddam Hussein's army in Iraq.

Terrorists continued to kill innocent people in Iraq and elsewhere in the world after the election was held.

Terrorists used bombs and other means to kill people to try to prevent the Iraqi people from holding elections.

3. Have students copy the following and give them 5 to 10 minutes to write an answer:

Explain whether or not you think the terrorist attacks of September 11, 2001, changed America forever.

4. Have students read their answers to the class and discuss or draw a picture about George W. Bush or have students do both.

Chapter Eight

Overview of Advice

The advice I offer here is directed at both the regular teacher and the substitute teacher because of the partnership that exists between the two if substituting is to be successful. The advice is divided into two parts: "Advice to the Regular Teacher" and "Advice to the Substitute Teacher." That division seems to exhibit some degree of logic.

I expect that many regular teachers, as well as many substitutes, may be aware of much of what I advise. Then of course, there is the possibility that a savvy regular teacher or savvy substitute teacher may even disagree with what I advise. Heresy! Heaven forbid! Relax—I expect that. These are only suggestions.

I am not going to bombard you with a complete course of action for any substitute or regular teacher. I gave more detailed advice in my book *The Substitute Teaching Survival Guide, Grades 6–12: Emergency Lesson Plans and Essential Advice.* That was because I thought the age of the students required it.

This is not to say that I think the job of secondary teachers is harder than the job of elementary teachers. As I perceive it, the jobs of elementary teachers and secondary teachers are just different; both are hard and easy, depending on the circumstances of the individual teacher. The blending of the two, elementary and secondary, starts to take place somewhere around the fourth or fifth grade and continues on through the eighth or ninth grade. By tenth grade, students are usually definitely secondary, as grades K–3 are definitely elementary. At the elementary end of the spectrum, you nurture them. At the secondary end of the spectrum, you huddle over them less and give them more independence of thought and action.

Becoming less dependent on nurturing and becoming more responsible for one's own well-being is a necessary part of being educated. As students mature, teachers of all grade levels have to decide how much freedom of action to give them.

The greatest challenge comes to middle school teachers when students are clamoring for more freedom of action but don't have the necessary self-restraint to handle much freedom. Then, of course, there are all those hormonal changes. To complicate middle school even more, the students all want to be nurtured like little children and be independent adults—at the same time, of course.

Good gravy, Ms. Mavey, middle school is a complex challenge for any teacher. No wonder there are days when middle school teachers wander home and wonder if they live in the same universe as other adults.

Maybe that's it—middle school is an entirely different dimension that Einstein and even today's cosmologists haven't discovered. The last I heard, some scientists say there are eleven dimensions, rather than the traditionally assumed three or four. Let's throw in middle school as the twelfth dimension. Ah yes, the twelfth dimension of middle school, where fact and fiction blend, where Big Foot inhabits the Bermuda Triangle, where it is hard to tell the good guys from the bad guys because they don't wear white hats, or any hats.

But the twelfth dimension does have its rewards as well as its challenges. Some teachers meet all of the challenges of the twelfth dimension and wouldn't choose to be anywhere else. It is particularly rewarding to a teacher who is able to take the immature students who come into middle school and guide them safely through that difficult period in their lives.

Whether a teacher teaches in elementary, middle, or high school, there is rarely a shortage of advice from education experts and others. Some of the advice is worthwhile; some of it is not. My advice is succinct and I hope useful. Take what you find worthy and discard what you feel is of no value.

Chapter Nine

Advice to the Regular Teacher

Suggestion 1: Be Concise in Your Instructions to the Sub

How much preparation you have to do when you're expecting a substitute depends on your own particular teaching situation and what the school has done to prepare for substitutes. Many schools provide a substitute folder at check-in time. If the office secretary does not give out a substitute folder and merely says to the substitute, "Sign this sheet and go to room 4-B," then you are elected to provide the substitute with the necessary basic information of time schedule, rest room locations, time to eat lunch, discipline procedures, and so on, that your substitute will need. Some schools have given each teacher a substitute folder that provides this type of information. The teacher merely leaves it in the room in the center desk drawer or some other permanent location where it can't disappear (or at least shouldn't disappear) and where the substitute can easily access it.

Whether you provide the basic information or the school provides it, anything that a sub is expected to read should be concise. A substitute doesn't have time to read *War and Peace*. The sub doesn't need to know the school's or your own philosophy of education. The sub just needs to know the things that will enable him or her to function in your class and at the school on a temporary basis.

Suggestion 2: Leave Lesson Plans That Are Easy for a Sub to Follow

The lesson plan should be concise (there's that word again). The lesson plan should not be too complex, and it should not be so demanding of a sub's attention that the sub can't monitor student behavior. Don't expect the sub to do the "loop the loop" or whatever it is that you can finesse with the skill of an ice skater who awes the judges at the Olympics.

Leave a lesson plan in concise (the word again), simple form that a sub can accomplish in an unfamiliar setting with unfamiliar students. You might even want the sub to do some of the exercises in this book. Of course, if the sub is a sub that you use a lot, who is totally familiar with how you teach, be as complex as you and the sub want.

Suggestion 3: Have a Seating Chart or Name Tags or Another Way for the Sub to Identify Each Student

A sub needs to know if students are required to sit in assigned seats. A sub needs to be able to identify each student by name.

I could give you all kinds of reasons for this suggestion, but you probably know the reasons already. If you don't, trust me. This is very important to a substitute.

Suggestion 4: Inform the Sub of the Procedure You Use to Let Students Go to the Rest Room

Students wanting to go to the bathroom can be a big headache for a sub. Your job, regular teacher, is not to let it be a headache for your sub. Inform your sub of the procedure for student bathroom use so that biological needs can be taken care of with a minimum of disruption to the class and to the sub.

Suggestion 5: Let the Sub Know, in Brief Form, What to Do if Student Misbehavior Goes Beyond What a Sub Can Normally Handle

Anticipate that there may be a student or students whose behavior becomes so bad that a sub can't cope with it. Leave the sub instructions on what is to be done to get misbehaving students under control. This might take the form of leaving a few simple instructions, such as the following:

> If a student misbehaves:
> 1. Tell the student you are going to turn his or her name in to me and the student will be in big trouble when I get back.
> 2. If the student continues to disrupt, get help from Ms. Carey in room next door (Room 5-C).
> 3. If that doesn't straighten the student out, call office extension 83 and ask Ms. Bright to come to class.

Subs usually know how to deal with most student misbehavior, but don't leave it entirely up to the sub to stand alone in withering fire from the few students who may become obnoxious. Remember, you and the sub are partners, even though you are not there. Provide the help your partner may need.

Suggestion 6: Leave Some Space on the Board for the Sub to Write

You never know what a sub may want to write on the board. It might even be some outrageous thing like "My name is Mr. Jarred. Sit down, please."

When a regular teacher has filled the board with something and has "SAVE" written all over the place, the regular teacher has deprived the sub of one of his or her most valuable tools. I know this is the electronic, computer, digital, high-definition, plug-it-in-and-hope-lightning-doesn't-strike age, but what wonderful educational tools chalkboards and felt-tipped pen boards have been and are.

Can't you just see one of those early men of learning chipping away at the bark on a tree as his male students sit cross-legged on the ground trying to decipher what it is the learned master is writing so they can dutifully scratch it onto their clay tablets? Thus was born learning and rote learning. Keep the tradition alive! Leave your sub some space to write on the board.

Suggestion 7: If Your Sub Is to Use Mechanical Equipment (VCR or Whatever), Have a Backup Plan in Case the Equipment Doesn't Work or Some Other Mishap Occurs

Don't leave a sub hanging with something like: "Sometime this morning get TV from Mr. Kojackel's room. I think he is in room 6, and he will probably be there if he is not in the faculty lounge or on supervision duty. You might check the lounge or the east end of the building if he is not in his room. I want you to show 'Willie Wonka's Wonka Momma,' which should be with the TV. Students will be fine. Let them sit anywhere and just have a party."

Of course, you being a great regular teacher, who knows how to help your subbing partner, will do a better job in making sure your sub gets the TV and the movie. You will provide better directions on how it is to be used. You will provide your sub with a backup plan (worksheet, vocabulary lesson, this book, or whatever) in case something happens and "Willie Wonka's Wonka Momma" can't be shown.

Suggestion 8: When Leaving a Lesson Plan That Requires Certain Students to Do Certain Things, Have a Backup Plan in Case Students Are Absent or for Some Other Reason Don't Participate

A backup plan is needed in case students are absent or for some other reason don't participate. If Madeline is the main character in the play and she is not there, the sub would find it very helpful if you had assigned Shelly to be her understudy. If the nurse has called half the class out to check for highly contagious earwax, wouldn't your sub like to have a backup lesson plan to use that doesn't require most members of the class to participate?

As I recommend in Suggestion 7, a worksheet, vocabulary lesson, this book, or whatever will suffice for a backup plan. You don't have to spend a lot of your valuable time constructing an intricate lesson plan. It's only the backup plan that may, but probably won't, be used.

Suggestion 9: Treat Subs with Respect

You know how you feel when somebody treats you as if you were at school to take out the dirty laundry, rather than respecting you as the professional that you are. Don't treat subs like dirty laundry. It won't make you feel good, and I can guarantee it won't make the sub you treat that way feel good. (By the way, no disrespect is intended to folks who work with dirty laundry. What kind of world would this be if nobody took care of dirty laundry?)

Remember that your substitute is your partner in education, your understudy who goes on when you can't perform, and by all means, the show must go on. Put it there, pals, we are all in this together, sink or swim, revive and survive, or whatever; you get the idea.

Suggestion 10: Use the Sub Report That You Receive as a Tool for Improvement

The report that the sub leaves you should be brief so that you, busy teacher, don't have a lot to read. You don't have time to read *War and Peace*.

But don't just shuck off the sub report as an inconsequential nuisance that has no relevance to what you do. There may be a kernel of an idea for improvement in that report. Use it to improve what happens the next time you have a sub.

If the sub report contains the name of an unruly student and the student suffers no consequences from misbehaving with the sub, don't be surprised when the student's misbehavior escalates with the next sub. If an unruly class hears nothing from the regular teacher about how they reduced the sub to tears, what is the next sub going to get? Burned at the stake?

Whether the sub comments on student behavior or something else, his or her comments may be worthy of your consideration as a basis for improving the situation for the next sub. Perhaps you need to change the type of lesson plan you provide. Maybe you need to be more specific in what you want the sub to do. Did you leave adequate instructions about bathroom breaks? Your partner is giving you valuable feedback. Take it seriously enough to drain whatever element of truth is in the report, and use it as a tool for improvement.

Chapter Ten

Advice to the Substitute Teacher

Suggestion 1: Have a Positive Attitude

Becoming the teacher for even 1 day can be a frightening experience, even when you are an experienced substitute. There is fear of the unknown: What kind of a classroom am I stepping into? Will the students be cooperative? Has the teacher left me something that is reasonable to do? Maybe I should have just stayed in bed, pulled the covers over my head, and mumbled, "Forget it. I'm not subbing today."

Relax. As we so often tell the students and say about many things in life, it's attitude. Go in with a good attitude, and good things may happen.

In my mind I can hear some substitute saying, "Oh sure, just when I thought this guy might know something about substituting, he comes out with something dumb like 'Expect some good things to happen.' It's a jungle out there, and the students are wild animals waiting to crunch my bones."

I can understand how a substitute might feel that way, but isn't it better to expect skipping through clover rather than expecting ghouls and goblins to whisk you away to never-never land, where torture begins first thing in the morning and doesn't end until the last bell of the day? Sometimes we get what we expect because we expect it.

Students immediately pick up on your attitude toward what you are doing and how you feel about them. A positive attitude that builds cooperation between you and the students can carry you a long way through the day. Yes, you can be stern and tough if you have to, but start out expecting a good day, and it may just be that way all through the day.

Suggestion 2: Let the Students Help You When It Is Appropriate and to Your Advantage

Elementary students usually love to be helpful, at least until they start showing signs of becoming middle school students. Even then, most will be helpful.

"It says on this paper Ms. Markus left me that I've got to let some people go to specials while others stay here and work on math problems, but she didn't tell me who is supposed to go when. Let's see the hands of who is supposed to go to specials. Well, that's interesting, the whole class. Who is going to help me know who goes when? Thanks for everybody volunteering, but I only need 2 people. I'm going to choose Belinda and Tyler. Belinda and Tyler, come up here for a minute and help me figure this out. Everybody else keep working on story time. Isn't that a nice story?"

Maybe that is where your positive attitude comes in. If you came in like a bear and growled at them first thing, and have been growling ever since, who is going to want to help you know or do anything?

Suggestion 3: Take a Pad of Sticky-Tabs with You

A good teacher will have left you a seating chart or name tags to identify the students. You need to be able to identify individual students to gain their cooperation, as well as to approve good behavior and chastise bad behavior.

In case the regular teacher has not left you a seating chart or some other means of identifying each student, pull out your pad of sticky-tabs and say something like, "I'm going to give each of you a sticky-tab to write your name on. Put it on the front of you so that I'll get to know you. What kind of day would it be if we spent the whole day together and we didn't even know each other? As you can see, I've written my name on the board so that you will know me."

Suggestion 4: Follow the Procedures and Lesson Plan of the Regular Teacher as Much as Possible

The regular teacher knows the students much better than you do and has conditioned them to respond in certain ways. Use to your advantage what your partner, the regular teacher, has put in place. The students will let you know about procedures: "This is how Ms. Mabeline has us line up when we go to lunch. If you're noisy she makes you go to the end of the line. Bobby always has to go to the end of the line, but I never do, because I'm good."

Elementary teachers are wonderful at having their own special ways of getting students quiet. Maybe it is standing in a special place so that the students know everybody is to be quiet except the teacher. Maybe it is holding up a hand and counting to 4 or 5 as each finger is lowered until the thumb finally shuts in all the fingers and everybody is supposed to be quiet. Use the expertise of your partner, the regular teacher, to your advantage.

Follow the regular teacher's lesson plan if at all possible. You are not here to do your own thing in any way that you want to. The regular teacher has things he or she wants you to teach. Try it his or her way, unless his way or her way is completely unworkable.

If there is no lesson plan, or the lesson plan has gaps of time, or the regular teacher has left a plan that makes it impossible to control the students, then you may have to use something you have devised. Of course, you could decide to use a lesson plan or lesson plans in this book. Holy moly! Why do you think this book was written? Could it be to help out at times when there is no lesson plan or the lesson plan has gone completely kaput? Yes, this book was published as an act of charity to help teachers who are in trouble.

Suggestion 5: Use Positive and Negative Recognition to Encourage Good Behavior and Discourage Bad Behavior

With your positive attitude that has produced charming little ladies and gentlemen, you are having a fine day. What's that, a dark cloud of unruly behavior floating over the room and settling on students? Defiance is rearing its ugly little head, whatever that would look like.

Students are refusing to cooperate. They are more interested in talking to each other than in paying attention to what you are saying. They are ignoring you! Whoops! There goes another one crawling on the floor to bite the leg of another student. Some students are starting to shoot wads of paper into the wastebasket. Now some students are leaning against the wall, casually smoking cigarettes, flipping the butts into the wastebasket to set the wads of paper on fire. A gang fight breaks out between the paper-wad shooters and the smokers. Paper-wad shooters are very sensitive about having their make-believe basketballs set on fire. You frantically try to decide whether to call the office for help or throw your body over the flaming wastebasket in the hope of extinguishing the fire before the piercing scream of the smoke detector sounds and the room is drenched in water cascading from the overhead sprinklers. You opt for smothering the wastebasket fire with your body, hoping that your gallant effort will gain you the special recognition you have always wanted: "Substitute Teacher of the Year."

Relax. It never happened. It never happened, because you were alert to the ripples of misbehavior before you had to shoot the rapids in an out-of-control classroom. You used the board to write the names of a couple of students who started to get out of control. You let them know that they could get their names off after 10 minutes or so of good behavior and their names wouldn't be turned in to the regular teacher if they continued to behave themselves.

Maybe there were a number of students who started misbehaving and you decided to start your "good list":

"I'm starting my good list. You want to get your name on it, because when Mr. Malarkey comes back, he will probably be very unhappy with the people who aren't on it. Nobody is on it yet, but when I think that you have demonstrated the kind of conduct and effort for a long enough time to put you on my good list, I'll bring my list to you for you to sign. It takes a while, and it won't be easy to get on it, but I think most of you will make it. Once you are on it, don't get knocked off by bad behavior. And don't ask me when you are going to get on it or tell me you have been good long enough that you should be on it. If you do that, your time needed to get on the list starts over. Don't worry; I'll be around to see you and will let you sign the list if you are doing a good job of behaving yourself and doing your work."

Any kind of recognition of good and bad behavior will usually work. Maybe it is writing the names of the "Super Good Guys" on the board, maybe it is writing the names of students whose behavior is "Not Appropriate Behavior" on the board, maybe it is the "good list" or something similar. In any case, don't let bad behavior slide into classroom chaos. You don't have to jump on every little thing students do, but find a balance between what you want to tolerate and keeping the class on the learning track.

I don't recommend taking candy or other treats to pass out to students for good behavior, because it may violate school policy or undercut the regular teacher's way of conducting class. Besides, do you want students to think of you as the "candy man" or "candy woman"? Surely, as teachers, we aspire to something higher than being classroom Santas? Don't we?

Suggestion 6: Use the Teacher's or the School's Backup Discipline Policy If Your Methods of Maintaining Control Don't Work

A good school will not put you totally on your own. "What's wrong? You're a sub; you are supposed to know how to handle any situation!" A good school and a good teacher will not leave you without any support in controlling students. Unfortunately, there are some schools that don't even give their regular teachers any support. Fortunately, they are probably the few, rather than the many.

If a student or the class is getting beyond your control, do whatever it is the teacher or school has recommended. Maybe it is seeking help from a team teacher. Maybe it is sending a student to the office. Maybe it is calling an administrator or counselor. Maybe it is sending the student to "time out" or some other place. Perhaps it is placing a student's name on the after-school detention list. Whatever it is, use it if necessary.

In my book on substituting in grades 6 to 12, I wrote that there might even be times when it is best for a substitute to leave an out-of-control classroom before the end of the period or before the end of the day. I recommended not leaving until an administrator, counselor, or some other regular staff member came to take over the class, so that legal consequences would not result from the substitute's departure.

I don't make the same recommendation for elementary schools. I don't see it happening in elementary that a class or students would be so out of control that a substitute would need to leave for his or her own safety or well-being.

Perhaps I'm being overly generous in my opinion of elementary schools and those who inhabit them, but I think students, staff, teachers, and administrators wouldn't let a substitute be run out of class by unruly students. I see elementary schools as places of nurturing, where teachers and all other adults work together much like family. Maybe I'm wrong about a sub never needing to "walk" from a classroom of misbehaving elementary students, but I don't think so.

Suggestion 7: Dress Appropriately

Take your cue from what the regular teachers wear. When you don't know that in advance, walk the line somewhere in the middle. Don't show up in high heels and an evening gown. Don't show up in sweats with a hole in the posterior, letting your posterior flab hang out. A tux is not necessary, nor should you show up in your dirty gray socks that you have worn all week long with your favorite band shirt with holes cut in the armpits.

Why dress appropriately? You will feel more comfortable blending in with the regular faculty, rather than standing out like a preening peacock or a Tasmanian devil, which by the way, some zoologists say is the smelliest animal on Earth when it gets agitated. (It is amazing the useful things you can learn from watching animal shows on television.)

Dress appropriately and the students will be more inclined to think of you as a regular member of the faculty, rather than a curiosity who happens to be spending the day with them. The regular faculty members will be more inclined to accept you as someone who knows something about teaching.

Suggestion 8: Take a Few Simple Measures to Increase Your Comfort Level

Now that you are properly dressed for substituting, permit me to make a few suggestions that might be of benefit to your level of comfort:

1. *Carry a bottle of water.*

   Who knows when you will ever be able to get a drink or even want to drink from the school drinking fountain?

2. *Carry cough drops or breath mints.*

   Have you ever started coughing or been unable to speak in the middle of a presentation because of a dry throat? Students find it disconcerting as they look at you, waiting for you to say something intelligent, rather than just staring at them as you point at your mouth where the lips are moving but no sound is coming out. Students today are pretty knowledgeable about first aid. You might find it disconcerting yourself when one of them grabs you in a Heimlich maneuver and another jumps you from the front and does mouth-to-mouth CPR.

3. *Carry a breakfast bar or fruit.* Or bring with you some other food that you can quickly ingest in case of a shortened lunch period or no lunch period.

4. *Plan for bathroom breaks.* Look at your schedule for the day and plan ahead for any bathroom breaks you may need. As a sub you may have a schedule that doesn't permit a bathroom break for yourself the entire morning, the entire afternoon, or the entire day. Good luck.

5. *Carry a jacket, sweater, or slip-on shirt.*

   Some rooms are chilly, some are hot. A little adjustment to your clothing can help, especially when you leave a warm room to stand bus duty or some other outside duty on a cold day.

6. *Give yourself enough time to arrive on time or even a little early.*

   Rushing into a classroom of waiting students can produce high anxiety (for you, not the students).

7. *Carry extra supplies.* Carry in your tote bag, or whatever you use to carry things, a few pencils and pieces of paper for your own use in case you need to fill out a bubble role sheet or do some other task that requires a pencil or paper and there is none.

8. *Carry a little notepad* or something to keep track of your substitute assignments and substitute dates.

   When you sub for a teacher, other teachers often ask you to sub for them: "I need a sub for next Tuesday. Are you available?" You pull out your little notepad from your pocket and say, "Let's see. I'm subbing at Fishbottom Elementary on Wednesday, but I haven't got anything on Tuesday. I'll be glad to sub for you. Let's see; it's Shirley Lovato—LOVAT O—and it's Tuesday, April 23. At what time? 7:30 it is. You call it in and I'll be here. I like coming here because this school always gives subs a free cookie. You know you get the best when you get a sub who works for cookies." (Sounds silly, but a school I subbed at quite a bit always gave each sub a chit for a giant cookie. I thought it was a nice gesture that showed that the school appreciated subs.)

9. *Forgive yourself when you don't do everything perfectly.* No matter how good a sub you are, you won't do everything right all the time. Don't expect perfection in yourself.

10. *When you have that occasional bad day, shrug it off and expect to have a good day the next time you sub.*

Suggestion 9: Make Your Report to the Regular Teacher Both Concise and Not Overly Critical

The regular teacher, getting ready for a day in the classroom, doesn't have time to read *War and Peace*. Yet, the regular teacher does need enough information to know what went on in his or her absence. Your job as a substitute is to inform the regular teacher of what he or she needs to know without being verbose and taking up time that the regular teacher needs to get ready for class.

Sometimes a few sentences will suffice:

> "We completed all the assignments you wanted completed. Class was very good. There were no problems and no troublemakers. Thanks for a nice day. Sincerely, Barton Bartholomew IV"

At other times you may need to say more, pointing out anomalies in the day (fire drill at 10:46), calling attention to work not completed (only got to problem 16 on math), leaving names of troublemakers (Jerico Weepingwillow and Filbert Foghorn were constantly talking to each other without permission), or giving other information that the regular teacher needs to know. The regular teacher will appreciate your being concise and relevant in your report.

It is inappropriate for you to pass judgment on the regular teacher's teaching skills, choice of subject matter, methods of discipline, and other things that are the prerogative of the regular teacher. You haven't been called in as an expert on teaching to instruct the regular teacher on how it should be done.

If you think there is something you must say, be diplomatic. Instead of "Your seating arrangement sucks!" maybe say, "I had a hard time keeping track of the students seated behind the large file cabinet. You probably know what they are doing, but as a sub I found it a little difficult to monitor their behavior." You made the point without offending. Furthermore, there may be a reason why the regular teacher seats them there, a reason you know nothing about.

Suggestion 10: Before Leaving at the End of the Day, Take a Few Minutes to Get Things in Order for the Regular Teacher

Remember that the regular teacher is your partner. You came in and worked a day, and now it is your partner's turn to come back in and work for a while. Taking a little time to tidy up the room a bit and put back in place anything you may have moved will be appreciated by your partner.

You appreciated it when you came in and everything was ready for you to take over the class: lesson plan in place, chalk or felt-tipped pen to write on the board, seating chart, and so on. Now it is time for you to return the favor. Make it easy for the regular teacher to pick up where you left off.

Whether it is tidying up the room or something else, follow the Golden Rule in your relationship with your partner. Don't go around bad-mouthing your partner to other teachers or administrators. Show your partner the same courtesy and respect that you deserve as a professional.

As a substitute you will have many partners. You will get to know some of your partners very well, and they will feel totally comfortable leaving their classes with you. Other partners you may only work with a time or 2. With mutual respect, whether it happens many times or only once, the partnership can be satisfying to both partners as we all get on with the noble task of educating children.

Epilogue

I have purposely not suggested a "bag of tricks." Although some substitutes may find puzzles, games, mind exercises, and other throw-in-quick activities valuable to fill spare moments or "downtime," they are not part of the curriculum. In my opinion, anything that takes away from following the curriculum and staying on target with prescribed learning is detrimental.

A "bag of tricks" may also foster the attitude that if the substitute does not like the prescribed lesson plan, the substitute can hurry through it and get to a "fun" activity of his or her choosing. Why should a substitute struggle with tough learning that students moan and groan over when the easy way out is to pull out the "bag of tricks"? The answer is because that is the substitute's job, just as it is the regular teacher's job, to stay focused on the curriculum and to make every moment count, whether the task is easy or difficult.

A "bag-of-tricks" attitude on the part of the regular teacher can be as bad as a "bag-of-tricks" attitude on the part of the substitute. It is the regular teacher's responsibility to leave in place a viable and valuable lesson plan for the substitute to follow. "Oh well, the substitute will have something to throw in if this doesn't work out" is a sloppy way to construct a lesson plan that is supposed to keep the students going in the curriculum where they should go.

As Ben Franklin said, "Waste not, want not." In my opinion, learning time is too valuable to waste on fill-in activities that don't follow the curriculum.

Of course, as always, I can stand corrected. If a "bag of tricks" increases the substitute's sense of security and it can be used effectively and enhances classroom learning, then by all means use it. For me, and maybe not you, I have found a "bag of tricks" more of a detriment to learning than a help.

It is my hope that the suggestions made in this book will be of value to you. Whether you are a substitute teacher or a regular teacher, I wish you every success in the noble purpose of educating our children.

Other Books of Interest

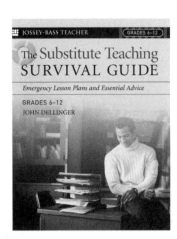

The Substitute Teaching Survival Guide, Grades 6–12: Emergency Lesson Plans and Essential Advice

John Dellinger

Paper ISBN: 0-7879-7411-0 144 pages
www.josseybass.com

When substitute teachers are assigned to a classroom, they often have no directions, no lesson plans, no information, and little hope of success. *The Substitute Teaching Survival Guide* offers substitute (and regular) teachers of grades 6–12 a welcome resource for planning and implementing a productive day of student learning.

The Substitute Teaching Survival Guide is filled with helpful suggestions and tips for maintaining order in the classroom and includes sixty-seven ready-to-use emergency lesson plans for language arts, mathematics, social studies, and science targeted for students in grades 6–12. Written for both the experienced and novice substitute teacher, the book also includes 152 suggestions and a daily outline of activities. The book can also be used by regular classroom teachers and principals who want to plan ahead for classroom absences, or by anyone who has to quickly cover a class.

Designed to be user-friendly, the book is organized into eleven chapters and printed in a lay-flat format. The chapters include:

- **The Role of the Substitute Teacher**
- **Discipline**
- **Lesson Plans**
- **Your Comfort Level**
- **The Importance of Substitute Teaching**
- **Is Substituting for You?**
- **Emergency Lesson Plans**
- **English Lesson Plans**
- **Math Lesson Plans**
- **Science Lesson Plans**
- **Social Studies Lesson Plans**

John Dellinger, a recipient of the Distinguished Teacher Award, is a retired Denver public school teacher who taught for twenty-eight years at the middle and high school levels. After retiring in 1992, he was a substitute teacher for seven years before shifting his major focus from teaching to writing.